KT-382-551

150
BAKING
recipes

INSPIRED IDEAS FOR
EVERYDAY COOKING

150
CAKE
recipes

INSPIRED IDEAS FOR
EVERYDAY COOKING

150
CHICKEN
recipes

INSPIRED IDEAS FOR
EVERYDAY COOKING

150
CUPCAKE
& MUFFIN
recipes

INSPIRED IDEAS FOR
EVERYDAY COOKING

150
FAST
& SIMPLE
recipes

INSPIRED IDEAS FOR
EVERYDAY COOKING

150
INDIAN
recipes

INSPIRED IDEAS FOR
EVERYDAY COOKING

150
PASTA
recipes

INSPIRED IDEAS FOR
EVERYDAY COOKING

150
SLOW
COOKER
recipes

INSPIRED IDEAS FOR
EVERYDAY COOKING

150
STIR-FRY
recipes

INSPIRED IDEAS FOR
EVERYDAY COOKING

150
STUDENT
recipes

INSPIRED IDEAS FOR
EVERYDAY COOKING

150
TAPAS
recipes

INSPIRED IDEAS FOR
EVERYDAY COOKING

150
VEGETARIAN
recipes

INSPIRED IDEAS FOR
EVERYDAY COOKING

150

CAKE
recipes

INSPIRED IDEAS FOR
EVERYDAY COOKING

CONTENTS

INTRODUCTION

How many of us can resist the enticing aroma of a freshly baked cake wafting from the kitchen? Home-made cakes are perfect for sharing with family, friends and colleagues and they evoke a wonderful feeling of contentment. Baking cakes is a popular pastime and it's certainly satisfying to munch your way through a cake you have just created and share it with others. Cakes make excellent edible gifts too. Simply wrapped in cellophane and tied with colourful ribbon or raffia, or presented in a pretty gift box, a home-baked cake will bring a smile to anyone's face.

We include a comprehensive collection of scrumptious cakes to suit all tastes and skill levels – from simple cakes to more sophisticated ones, there's a cake to suit every occasion! So, go and get a buzz from baking and enjoy creating some truly delicious cakes.

We begin by featuring some ever-popular classic cakes, including family favourites such as Carrot Cake, Lemon Drizzle Cake and Gingerbread, along with other temptations like Easy Apple Cake and Cherry Cake.

A brilliant book on cakes wouldn't be complete without a chapter featuring some choice chocolate cakes, ideal for all chocoholics. Indulge in delights such as Chocolate Ganache Cake, Mocha Slab Cake and Chocolate Swirl Loaf. Or, for festive family occasions, try a sumptuous Chocolate Yule Log or Sachertorte.

Next up is an inspiring selection of fruit and nut cakes, comprising creative crumb cakes, ring cakes, tray bakes, upside-down cakes, crunch cakes, spicy cakes, layer cakes and tea loaves. Choose from temptations like Pear & Pecan Sponge Cake, Blueberry Tray Bake and Blood Orange Polenta Cake.

Not forgetting just how popular mini cakes are, our next chapter encompasses an appealing collection of small and mini cakes, perfect for parties, afternoon teas, office breaks or get-togethers. Try your hand at baking a batch of cupcakes, whoopie pies, mini loaf cakes, mini Bundt cakes, cake pops or muffins. Among these sensational treats are Home-made Jaffa Cakes and Beetroot Brownie Bites.

Last, but by no means least, we include an assortment of delectable dessert cakes, all of which are sure to impress. Our superb choice of cheesecakes, roulades, tortes and gateaux include moreish Mocha Cheesecake, Walnut Torte and Caramel Peach Gateau.

For those with special dietary requirements, we include some tempting cakes that will satisfy their sweet cravings too. Suitable choice recipes include Gluten-Free Chocolate Fudge Cake, Vegan Chocolate & Raspberry Cake, Gluten-Free Carrot Cake and Wheat, Gluten and Dairy-free Banana Cake.

If your cake-making skills are a little rusty, then start with something straightforward like a Victoria Sponge Cake, Butterfly Cakes or No Bake Chocolate Refrigerator Cake.

As you gradually become more savvy and confident in the kitchen and find your cake-making competence, try more elaborate creations such as Chocolate & Orange Ring Cake, Vanilla & Rose Macaroons or Rich Chocolate Torte. You'll be surprised and delighted at how soon you'll be baking impressive cakes!

You don't need a lot of specialist equipment for making cakes and you are likely to already have most things you will need. Basic equipment such as good quality baking tins (in various shapes and sizes), a reliable set of kitchen scales, a good set of mixing bowls and a couple of spatulas and wooden spoons are useful to have before you embark on your baking quest. An electric hand-held mixer or a stand mixer will also prove invaluable.

And remember, when making cakes, it's particularly important to weigh out all your ingredients carefully and have them prepared and ready to use before you begin a recipe. Also, don't forget to preheat the oven before you start!

INTRODUCTION

CLASSIC FAVOURITES

CARROT CAKE

Serves: 6

Prep: 30 mins, plus cooling

Cook: 35–40 mins

Ingredients

butter, for greasing
100 g/3½ oz self-raising flour
pinch of salt
1 tsp ground mixed spice
½ tsp ground nutmeg
125 g/4½ oz soft light brown sugar
2 eggs, beaten
5 tbsp sunflower oil
125 g/4½ oz carrots, grated
1 banana, chopped
25 g/1 oz chopped toasted mixed nuts

Frosting

40 g/1½ oz butter, softened
3 tbsp cream cheese
175 g/6 oz icing sugar
1 tsp fresh orange juice
grated rind of ½ orange
walnut halves or pieces, to decorate

Method

1 Preheat the oven to 180°C/350°F/Gas Mark 4. Grease an 18-cm/7-inch square cake tin and line with baking paper.

2 Sift the flour, salt, mixed spice and nutmeg into a bowl. Stir in the brown sugar, then stir in the eggs and oil. Add the carrots, banana and nuts and mix well together.

3 Spoon the mixture into the prepared tin. Bake in the preheated oven for 35–40 minutes, or until risen, golden and springy to the touch. Leave to cool slightly, then transfer to a wire rack to cool completely.

4 To make the frosting, put the butter, cream cheese, icing sugar and orange juice and rind in a bowl and beat together until creamy. Spread the frosting over the top of the cake, then use a fork to make wavy lines in the frosting. Scatter over the walnuts and cut the cake into six pieces.

★ **Variation**

For a different, more zingy flavoured frosting, swap the orange juice and rind for lime juice and rind instead.

CLASSIC FAVOURITES

CHOCOLATE CAKE

Serves: 10

Prep: 35 mins,
plus cooling & chilling

Cook: 30–35 mins

Ingredients

55 g/2 oz cocoa powder

7 tbsp boiling water

200 g/7 oz butter, softened, plus extra for greasing

125 g/4½ oz caster sugar

70 g/2½ oz soft light brown sugar

4 eggs, beaten

1 tsp vanilla extract

200 g/7 oz self-raising flour

Frosting

200 g/7 oz plain chocolate, broken into pieces

115 g/4 oz butter

100 ml/3½ fl oz double cream

Method

1 Preheat the oven to 180°C/350°F/Gas Mark 4. Grease two 20-cm/8-inch sandwich tins and line with baking paper.

2 Blend the cocoa powder and water to a smooth paste and set aside. Put the butter, caster sugar and brown sugar into a large bowl and beat together until light and creamy. Gradually beat in the eggs, then stir in the cocoa paste and vanilla extract.

3 Sift in the flour and fold in gently. Divide the mixture evenly between the prepared tins and smooth the surfaces. Bake in the preheated oven for 25–30 minutes, or until risen and springy to the touch. Leave to cool slightly, then transfer to a wire rack to cool completely.

4 To make the frosting, put the chocolate and butter into a heatproof bowl set over a saucepan of simmering water and heat until melted. Remove from the heat and stir in the cream. Leave to cool for 20 minutes, then chill in the refrigerator for 40–50 minutes, stirring occasionally, until thick enough to spread.

5 Sandwich the cakes together with one third the frosting, then spread the remainder over top and sides of the cake.

COFFEE & WALNUT CAKE

Serves: 8

Prep: 35 mins, plus cooling

Cook: 20–25 mins

Ingredients

175 g/6 oz butter, softened, plus extra for greasing

175 g/6 oz light muscovado sugar

3 large eggs, beaten

3 tbsp strong black coffee

175 g/6 oz self-raising flour

1½ tsp baking powder

115 g/4 oz walnut pieces

walnut halves, to decorate

Frosting

115 g/4 oz butter, softened

200 g/7 oz icing sugar

1 tbsp strong black coffee

½ tsp vanilla extract

Method

1 Preheat the oven to 180°C/350°F/Gas Mark 4. Grease two 20-cm/8-inch sandwich tins and line with baking paper.

2 Beat the butter and muscovado sugar together until light and creamy. Gradually add the eggs, beating well after each addition. Beat in the coffee.

3 Sift the flour and baking powder into the mixture, then fold in lightly and evenly with a metal spoon. Fold in the walnut pieces. Divide the mixture evenly between the prepared tins and smooth the surfaces. Bake in the preheated oven for 20–25 minutes, or until risen and springy to the touch. Leave to cool slightly, then transfer to a wire rack to cool completely.

4 To make the frosting, beat together the butter, icing sugar, coffee and vanilla extract until smooth and creamy.

5 Use about half of the frosting to sandwich the cakes together, then spread the remaining frosting on top and swirl with a palette knife. Decorate with walnut halves.

CLASSIC FAVOURITES

ANGEL FOOD CAKE

Serves: 10

Prep: 25 mins,
plus cooling

Cook: 45-50 mins

Ingredients

sunflower oil, for greasing
8 large egg whites
1 tsp cream of tartar
1 tsp almond extract
250 g/9 oz caster sugar
115 g/4 oz plain flour,
plus extra for dusting

To decorate

250 g/9 oz summer berries
1 tbsp lemon juice
2 tbsp icing sugar

Method

1 Preheat the oven to 160°C/325°F/Gas Mark 3. Grease and lightly flour a 24-cm/9½-inch ring tin.

2 In a clean, grease-free bowl, whisk the egg whites until they hold soft peaks. Add the cream of tartar and whisk again until the whites are stiff but not dry. Whisk in the almond extract, then add the caster sugar, a tablespoon at a time, whisking hard between each addition. Sift in the flour and fold in lightly and evenly using a large metal spoon.

3 Spoon the mixture into the prepared tin. Bake in the preheated oven for 40–45 minutes, or until risen, golden and springy to the touch. Run the tip of a knife around the edges of the cake to loosen from the tin. Leave to cool slightly, then transfer to a wire rack to cool completely.

4 To decorate, place the berries, lemon juice and icing sugar in a saucepan and heat until the sugar has dissolved. Spoon over the cake.

CLASSIC FAVOURITES

GINGER OAT CAKE

Serves: 10–12

Prep: 20 mins, plus cooling & storing

Cook: 1 hour 50 mins– 2 hours 5 mins

Ingredients

150 g/5½ oz self-raising flour
pinch of salt
½ tsp ground mixed spice
2 tsp ground ginger
200 g/7 oz oatmeal
175 g/6 oz black treacle
100 g/3½ oz butter, plus extra for greasing
85 g/3 oz soft brown sugar
1 tbsp milk
1 egg, beaten

Method

1 Preheat the oven to 140°C/275°F/Gas Mark 1. Grease a 15-cm/6-inch square cake tin and line with baking paper.

2 Sift the flour into a large bowl and stir in the salt, spices and oatmeal. Make a well in the centre.

3 Place the treacle, butter and sugar in a saucepan and melt slowly over a low heat, without allowing the mixture to boil. Pour the melted mixture into the well of the dry ingredients and gently combine. Stir in the milk and egg and mix until smooth.

4 Spoon the mixture into the prepared tin. Bake in the preheated oven for 1¾–2 hours, or until risen and springy to the touch.

5 Leave to cool slightly, then transfer to a wire rack to cool completely. Store in an airtight container in a cool place for at least a week before cutting and serving, to allow it to become moist and sticky.

VICTORIA SPONGE CAKE

Serves: 8–10

Prep: 25 mins, plus cooling

Cook: 25–30 mins

Ingredients

175 g/6 oz butter, softened, plus extra for greasing

175 g/6 oz caster sugar

3 eggs, beaten

175 g/6 oz self-raising flour

pinch of salt

3 tbsp raspberry jam

1 tbsp caster or icing sugar

Method

1 Preheat the oven to 180°C/350°F/Gas Mark 4. Grease two 20-cm/8-inch sandwich tins and line with baking paper.

2 Beat the butter and sugar together in a large bowl until light and creamy. Add the eggs a little at a time, beating well after each addition. Sift in the flour and salt and fold in gently with a metal spoon.

3 Divide the mixture evenly between the prepared tins and smooth the surfaces. Bake in the preheated oven for 25–30 minutes, or until risen, golden and springy to the touch.

4 Leave to cool slightly, then transfer to a wire rack to cool completely.

5 When completely cool, sandwich the cakes together with the jam and sprinkle the sugar evenly over the top of the cake.

CLASSIC FAVOURITES

CHOCOLATE FUDGE CAKE

Serves: 8

Prep: 35 mins,
plus cooling & chilling

Cook: 35–40 mins

Ingredients

175 g/6 oz butter, softened, plus extra for greasing

175 g/6 oz golden caster sugar

3 eggs, beaten

3 tbsp golden syrup

0 g/1½ oz ground almonds

175 g/6 oz self-raising flour

pinch of salt

40 g/1½ oz cocoa powder

Frosting

225 g/8 oz plain chocolate, broken into pieces

5 g/2 oz muscovado sugar

225 g/8 oz butter, diced

5 tbsp evaporated milk

½ tsp vanilla extract

Method

1 Preheat the oven to 180°C/350°F/Gas Mark 4. Grease two 20-cm/8-inch sandwich tins and line with baking paper.

2 To make the frosting, place the chocolate, muscovado sugar, butter, evaporated milk and vanilla extract in a saucepan. Heat gently, stirring constantly, until melted. Pour into a bowl and leave to cool. Cover and chill in the refrigerator for 1 hour, or until spreadable.

3 For the cake, place the butter and caster sugar in a large bowl and beat together until light and creamy. Gradually beat in the eggs. Stir in the golden syrup and ground almonds. Sift the flour, salt and cocoa powder into a separate bowl, then fold into the mixture. Add a little water, if necessary, to make a dropping consistency.

4 Divide the mixture evenly between the prepared tins and smooth the surfaces. Bake in the preheated oven for 30–35 minutes, or until risen and springy to the touch.

5 Leave to cool slightly, then transfer to a wire rack to cool completely. When the cakes are cool, sandwich them together with half of the frosting. Spread the remaining frosting over the top and sides of the cake, swirling it to give a frosted appearance.

CLASSIC FAVOURITES

EASY APPLE CAKE

Serves: 8

Prep: 25 mins, plus cooling

Cook: 45–50 mins

Ingredients

400 g/14 oz eating apples, peeled, cored and diced

2 tbsp apple juice

140 g/5 oz light muscovado sugar

125 g/4½ oz butter, softened, plus extra for greasing

2 large eggs, beaten

225 g/8 oz self-raising flour

1½ tsp ground mixed spice

40 g/1½ oz hazelnuts, peeled and finely chopped

Method

1 Preheat the oven to 190°C/375°F/Gas Mark 5. Grease a 20-cm/8-inch round cake tin and line with baking paper. Sprinkle the apples with the apple juice and set aside.

2 Reserve 1 tablespoon of the sugar, then place the sugar and butter into a large bowl and beat until light and creamy. Gradually add the eggs, beating thoroughly after each addition. Sift together the flour and spice into the mixture and evenly fold in with a metal spoon.

3 Stir the apples and juice into the mixture. Spoon the mixture into the prepared tin. Mix the hazelnuts with the reserved sugar and sprinkle over the surface of the cake.

4 Bake in the preheated oven for 45–50 minutes, or until risen, golden and springy to the touch. Leave to cool slightly, then transfer to a wire rack to cool completely.

LEMON DRIZZLE CAKE

Serves: 8

Prep: 20 mins, plus cooling

Cook: 45–60 mins

Ingredients

butter, for greasing
200 g/7 oz plain flour
2 tsp baking powder
200 g/7 oz caster sugar
4 eggs
150 ml/5 fl oz soured cream
grated rind of 1 large lemon
4 tbsp lemon juice
150 ml/5 fl oz sunflower oil

Syrup

4 tbsp icing sugar
3 tbsp lemon juice

Method

1 Preheat the oven to 180°C/350°F/Gas Mark 4. Grease a 20-cm/8-inch round cake tin and line with baking paper.

2 Sift the flour and baking powder into a large bowl and stir in the caster sugar.

3 In a separate bowl, whisk the eggs, soured cream, lemon rind, lemon juice and oil together.

4 Pour the egg mixture into the dry ingredients and mix well until evenly combined.

5 Spoon the mixture into the prepared tin and bake in the preheated oven for 45–60 minutes, or until risen, golden and springy to the touch.

6 Meanwhile, to make the syrup, mix together the icing sugar and lemon juice in a small saucepan. Stir over a low heat until just beginning to bubble and turn syrupy.

7 As soon as the cake comes out of the oven, prick the surface with a fine skewer, then brush the syrup over the top. Leave the cake to cool completely in the tin before turning out and serving.

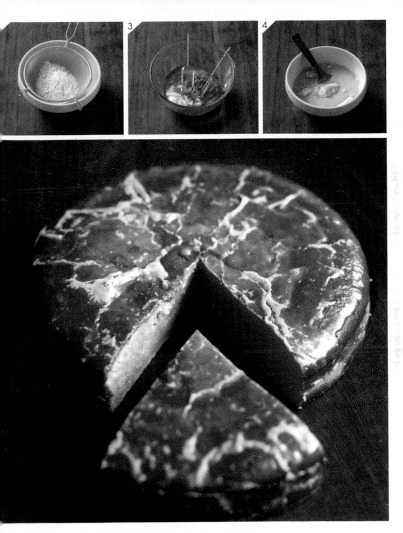

ICED GINGERBREAD

Serves: 12

Prep: 30 mins,
plus cooling & setting

Cook: 1 hour 5 mins–
1 hour 20 mins

Ingredients

250 g/9 oz plain flour

1 tsp bicarbonate of soda

1½ tsp ground ginger

1 tsp ground mixed spice

115 g/4 oz butter,
plus extra for greasing

115 g/4 oz light muscovado
sugar

150 g/5½ oz golden syrup

85 g/3 oz black treacle

2 large eggs, beaten

2 tbsp milk

Icing

115 g/4 oz icing sugar

1 tbsp stem
ginger syrup

1–2 tbsp water

1 piece stem ginger,
finely chopped

Method

1 Preheat the oven to 160°C/325°F/Gas Mark 3.
Grease an 18-cm/7-inch square cake tin and
line with baking paper.

2 Sift the flour, bicarbonate of soda, ground ginger
and mixed spice into a large bowl. Place the
butter, sugar, golden syrup and black treacle in
a saucepan and heat gently, stirring all the time,
until the butter has melted. Cool for 5 minutes.

3 Stir the melted mixture into the bowl and mix
well. Add the eggs and milk and beat until
thoroughly incorporated.

4 Spoon the mixture into the prepared tin and
bake in the preheated oven for 1–1¼ hours, or
until risen and springy to the touch. Leave to
cool slightly, then transfer to a wire rack to cool
completely.

5 For the icing, sift the icing sugar into a bowl. Stir in
the stem ginger syrup and enough of the water
to make a smooth icing that just coats the back
of a wooden spoon.

6 Spoon the icing over the top of the cake,
allowing it to run down the sides. Scatter over the
stem ginger and leave to set.

CLASSIC FAVOURITES

WHEAT, GLUTEN & DAIRY-FREE PEAR CAKE

Serves: 12

Prep: 30 mins, plus cooling

Cook: 55–60 mins

Ingredients

175 g/6 oz dairy-free spread, plus extra for greasing

175 g/6 oz caster sugar

3 large eggs, beaten

½ tsp vanilla extract

175 g/6 oz gluten- and wheat-free plain flour

2 tsp gluten- and wheat-free baking powder

½ tsp ground cinnamon

30 g/1 oz ground almonds

500 g/1 lb 2 oz canned pear halves, drained

Crumble topping

150 g/5½ oz gluten- and wheat-free plain flour

115 g/4 oz dairy-free spread

50 g/1¾ oz caster sugar

1 handful of flaked almonds

Method

1 Preheat the oven to 180°C/350°F/Gas Mark 4. Grease a 20-cm/8-inch round cake tin and line with baking paper.

2 Beat the spread and sugar together in a large bowl until fluffy. Add the eggs gradually, one at a time, mixing well, then add the vanilla extract and stir. Sift in the flour, baking powder and cinnamon, and fold gently into the mixture. Add the ground almonds and fold in.

3 Spoon the mixture into the prepared tin and place the pear halves evenly on top, pushing them down a little.

4 To make the crumble topping, put the flour, spread and sugar into a bowl and rub together, using your fingertips, to form the crumble. Sprinkle the crumble mixture over the top of the cake and sprinkle with the flaked almonds.

5 Bake in the preheated oven for 55–60 minutes, or until risen and golden. Leave to cool slightly, then transfer to a wire rack to cool completely.

WARM GREEK YOGURT & HONEY CAKE

Serves: 6–8

Prep: 20 mins, plus cooling

Cook: 50–60 mins

Ingredients

oil or melted butter, for greasing
175 g/6 oz plain flour
1 tbsp baking powder
175 g/6 oz Greek-style yogurt
100 g/3½ oz honey
75 g/2½ oz light muscovado sugar
3 eggs, beaten
1 tsp vanilla extract

Lemon sauce
2 tbsp honey
2 tbsp lemon juice
25 g/1 oz butter

Method

1 Preheat the oven to 160°C/325°F/Gas Mark 3. Grease a 23-cm/9-inch round cake tin and line with baking paper.

2 Sift the flour and baking powder into a large bowl and add the yogurt, honey, sugar, eggs and vanilla extract. Beat well until the mixture is smooth.

3 Spoon the mixture into the prepared tin. Bake in the preheated oven for 45–55 minutes, or until risen, golden and springy to the touch. Leave to cool slightly, then transfer to a serving plate.

4 To make the lemon sauce, place the honey, lemon juice and butter in a small saucepan and bring to the boil. Boil for a few minutes, stirring, until reduced and syrupy.

5 Serve the cake in slices with the lemon sauce poured over.

CLASSIC FAVOURITES

COFFEE CRUMB CAKE

Serves: 8-10

Prep: 30 mins,
plus cooling

Cook: 55-60 mins

Ingredients

225 g/8 oz plain flour

1 tbsp baking powder

70 g/2½ oz caster sugar

150 ml/5 fl oz milk

2 eggs

115 g/4 oz butter, melted,
plus extra for greasing

2 tbsp strong coffee

50 g/1¾ oz chopped
almonds

icing sugar, for dusting

Topping

70 g/2½ oz self-raising flour

0 g/2½ oz demerara sugar

2 tbsp butter, diced

1 tsp ground mixed spice

1 tbsp water

Method

1 Preheat the oven to 190°C/375°F/Gas Mark 5.
Grease a 23-cm/9-inch round cake tin and line
with baking paper.

2 Sift the plain flour and baking powder into a
large bowl, then stir in the caster sugar.

3 Whisk the milk, eggs, melted butter and coffee
together and pour over the dry ingredients. Add
the chopped almonds and mix lightly together.
Spoon the mixture into the prepared tin.

4 To make the topping, mix the self-raising flour
and demerara sugar together in a bowl. Rub in
the butter with your fingertips until the mixture
resembles breadcrumbs. Sprinkle in the mixed
spice and add the water and bring the mixture
together until it resembles loose crumbs. Sprinkle
the topping evenly over the cake mixture.

5 Bake in the preheated oven for 50-55 minutes, or
until risen and springy to the touch. Cover loosely
with foil in case the topping browns too quickly.

6 Leave to cool slightly, then transfer to a wire rack
to cool completely. Dust with icing sugar just
before serving.

CLASSIC FAVOURITES

BANANA & WALNUT LOAF

Serves: 10

Prep: 20 mins,
plus cooling

Cook: 1 hour

Ingredients

250 g/9 oz plain flour

1½ tsp baking powder

200 g/7 oz light muscovado sugar

55 g/2 oz chopped walnuts

2 large eggs

100 ml/3½ fl oz sunflower oil, plus extra for greasing

2 ripe bananas, mashed

100 ml/3½ fl oz milk

1 tsp vanilla extract

8 walnut halves

Method

1 Preheat the oven to 180°C/350°F/Gas Mark 4. Grease a 900-g/2-lb loaf tin and line with baking paper.

2 Sift together the flour and baking powder into a large bowl and stir in the sugar and chopped walnuts.

3 Put the eggs, oil, bananas, milk and vanilla extract into a bowl and beat together, then stir into the dry ingredients and mix together.

4 Spoon the mixture into the prepared tin and smooth the surface. Arrange the walnut halves over the surface.

5 Bake in the preheated oven for about 1 hour, or until risen, golden and springy to the touch. Leave to cool slightly, then transfer to a wire rack to cool completely.

GLUTEN-FREE STICKY FRUIT LOAF

Serves: 10

Prep: 25 mins,
plus soaking & cooling

Cook: 1¼–1¾ hours

Ingredients

350 g/12 oz sultanas

zest and juice of 1 lemon

220 g/7¾ oz butter, softened, plus extra for greasing

220 g/7¾ oz dark soft brown sugar

½ tsp glycerine

5 eggs, beaten

250 g/9 oz gluten-free, wheat-free plain flour

2 tsp ground mixed spice

3 tbsp black treacle

2 tbsp gluten-free whiskey

g/2¼ oz ground almonds

60 g/2¼ oz glacé cherries

60 g/2¼ oz mixed seeds (e.g. sunflower, sesame, millet)

Method

1 Mix the sultanas with the lemon zest and juice and 4 tablespoons of warm water. Mix well and leave to soak for an hour or until plump.

2 Preheat the oven to 150°C/300°F/Gas Mark 2. Grease a 900-g/2-lb loaf tin and line with baking paper.

3 Beat the butter, sugar and glycerine in a large bowl. Add the eggs, one at a time, and stir in. Add the rest of the ingredients, including the dried fruits with their soaking liquid, to the bowl and mix well.

4 Spoon the mixture into the prepared tin. Bake in the preheated oven for 1¼–1¾ hours, or until risen, golden and springy to the touch.

5 Leave to cool slightly, then transfer to a wire rack to cool completely. This loaf improves with age, so make it the day before you want to serve it for a really sticky, moist loaf.

CLASSIC FAVOURITES

VANILLA SPONGE CAKE

Serves: 8

Prep: 25–30 mins, plus cooling

Cook: 20–25 mins

Ingredients

225 g/8 oz plain flour

2 tsp baking powder

225 g/8 oz butter, softened, plus extra for greasing

225 g/8 oz caster sugar

4 eggs, beaten

1 tsp vanilla extract

coloured flower sprinkles, to decorate

Frosting

140 g/5 oz butter, softened

200 g/7 oz icing sugar

1 tsp vanilla extract

Method

1 Preheat the oven to 180°C/350°F/Gas Mark 4. Grease two 20-cm/8-inch sandwich tins and line with baking paper.

2 Sift together the flour and baking powder into a large bowl and add the butter, sugar, eggs and vanilla extract. Beat with an electric hand-held mixer until just smooth.

3 Divide the mixture evenly between the prepared tins and smooth the surfaces. Bake in the preheated oven for 20–25 minutes, or until risen, golden and springy to the touch.

4 Leave to cool slightly, then transfer to a wire rack to cool completely.

5 To make the frosting, put the butter, icing sugar and vanilla extract into a bowl and beat until smooth and spreadable. Use half of the frosting to sandwich the two cakes together.

6 Spread the remaining frosting over the top of the cake and decorate with flower sprinkles.

BANANA BREAD LOAF

Serves: 6

Prep: 20 mins,
plus cooling

Cook: 45 mins

Ingredients

225 g/8 oz vegetable fat, plus extra for greasing

90 g/3¼ oz sugar

150 g/5½ oz plain flour

3 tsp baking powder

1 tsp bicarbonate of soda

1 tsp salt

2 tbsp water

2 eggs, beaten

3 ripe bananas, mashed

Method

1 Preheat the oven to 160°C/325°F/Gas Mark 3. Grease a 450-g/1-lb loaf tin and line with baking paper.

2 Place the vegetable fat and sugar into a large bowl and beat together until light and creamy. Sift in the flour, baking powder, bicarbonate of soda and salt and fold in gently. Add the water and eggs and mix together to combine.

3 Add the mashed bananas and stir in. Spoon the mixture into the prepared tin. Use a spatula dipped in a little oil to score an impression along the centre of the loaf.

4 Bake in the preheated oven for 45 minutes, or until risen, golden and springy to the touch. Leave to cool slightly, then transfer to a wire rack to cool completely.

CHERRY CAKE

Serves: 8

Prep: 25 mins,
plus cooling

Cook: 1–1¼ hours

Ingredients

250 g/9 oz glacé cherries, quartered

85 g/3 oz ground almonds

200 g/7 oz plain flour

1 tsp baking powder

200 g/7 oz butter, softened, plus extra for greasing

200 g/7 oz caster sugar

3 large eggs, beaten

finely grated rind and juice of 1 lemon

6 sugar cubes, crushed

Method

1 Preheat the oven to 180°C/350°F/Gas Mark 4. Grease a 20-cm/8-inch round cake tin and line with baking paper.

2 Stir together the cherries, almonds and 1 tablespoon of the flour. Sift the remaining flour into a separate bowl with the baking powder.

3 Place the butter and sugar in a large bowl and beat together until light and creamy. Gradually add the eggs, beating hard, until evenly mixed.

4 Add the flour mixture and fold lightly and evenly into the creamed mixture with a metal spoon. Add the cherry mixture, fold in evenly, then fold in the lemon rind and juice.

5 Spoon the mixture into the prepared tin and sprinkle with the crushed sugar cubes. Bake in the preheated oven for 1–1¼ hours, or until risen, golden and springy to the touch.

6 Leave to cool slightly, then transfer to a wire rack to cool completely.

CLASSIC FAVOURITES

ALMOND CAKE

Serves: 8

Prep: 25 mins, plus cooling

Cook: 50–60 mins

Ingredients

butter, for greasing

250 g/9 oz ricotta cheese

4 eggs, separated

1 tsp almond extract

175 g/6 oz golden caster sugar

250 g/9 oz ground almonds

finely grated rind of 1 lime

toasted flaked almonds, to decorate

icing sugar, for dusting

Method

1 Preheat the oven to 150°C/300°F/Gas Mark 2. Grease a 23-cm/9-inch round cake tin and line with baking paper.

2 Beat together the ricotta, egg yolks, almond extract and caster sugar in a large bowl. Stir in the almonds and lime rind.

3 Whisk the egg whites in a clean, grease-free bowl until they form soft peaks.

4 Fold the whites lightly into the ricotta mixture, using a large metal spoon.

5 Spoon the mixture into the prepared tin and bake in the preheated oven for 50–60 minutes, or until risen, golden, and springy to the touch.

6 Leave to cool slightly, then transfer to a wire rack and sprinkle with flaked almonds. Leave to cool completely and dust with icing sugar.

CLASSIC FAVOURITES

RED VELVET CAKE

Serves: 12

Prep: 30 mins,
plus cooling

Cook: 30–35 mins

Ingredients

225 g/8 oz butter, plus extra
for greasing

4 tbsp water

55 g/2 oz cocoa powder

3 eggs, beaten

250 ml/9 fl oz buttermilk

2 tsp vanilla extract

2 tbsp red edible
food colouring

280 g/10 oz plain flour

55 g/2 oz cornflour

1½ tsp baking powder

280 g/10 oz caster sugar

Frosting

250 g/9 oz cream cheese

40 g/1½ oz butter, softened

3 tbsp caster sugar

1 tsp vanilla extract

Method

1 Preheat the oven to 190°C/375°F/Gas Mark 5.
Grease two 23-cm/9-inch sandwich tins and line
with baking paper.

2 Place the butter, water and cocoa powder in a
small saucepan and heat gently, without boiling,
stirring until melted and smooth. Remove from
the heat and leave to cool slightly.

3 Beat together the eggs, buttermilk, vanilla
extract and food colouring until frothy. Beat in
the butter mixture. Sift together the flour, cornflour
and baking powder, then stir quickly and evenly
into the mixture with the caster sugar.

4 Divide the mixture evenly between the prepared
tins and smooth the surfaces. Bake in the
preheated oven for 25–30 minutes, or until risen
and springy to the touch. Leave to cool slightly,
then transfer to a wire rack to cool completely.

5 To make the frosting, beat together all the
ingredients until smooth. Use about half of the
frosting to sandwich the cakes together, then
spread the remainder over the top, swirling with
a palette knife.

CLASSIC FRUIT CAKE

Serves: 16

Prep: 35 mins, plus soaking, cooling & storing

Cook: 2¼–2¾ hours

Ingredients

350 g/12 oz sultanas

225 g/8 oz raisins

115 g/4 oz ready-to-eat dried apricots, chopped

85 g/3 oz dates, stoned and chopped

4 tbsp dark rum or brandy, plus extra for flavouring (optional)

finely grated rind and juice of 1 orange

225 g/8 oz butter, softened, plus extra for greasing

225 g/8 oz light muscovado sugar

4 eggs, beaten

70 g/2½ oz chopped mixed peel

85 g/3 oz glacé cherries, quartered

25 g/1 oz chopped glacé ginger or stem ginger

40 g/1½ oz blanched almonds, chopped

200 g/7 oz plain flour

1 tsp ground mixed spice

Method

1 Place the sultanas, raisins, apricots and dates in a large bowl and stir in the rum, orange rind and orange juice. Cover and leave to soak for several hours or overnight.

2 Preheat the oven to 150°C/300°F/Gas Mark 2. Grease a 20-cm/8-inch deep round cake tin and line with baking paper.

3 Put the butter and sugar in a large bowl and beat together until light and creamy. Gradually beat in the eggs, beating after each addition. Stir in the soaked fruits, mixed peel, glacé cherries, glacé ginger and blanched almonds.

4 Sift in the flour and mixed spice, then fold lightly and evenly into the mixture. Spoon the mixture into the prepared tin, making a depression in the centre with the back of the spoon.

5 Bake in the preheated oven for 2¼–2¾ hours, or until risen and springy to the touch. Leave to cool slightly, then transfer to a wire rack to cool.

6 Wrap the cooled cake in greaseproof paper and foil. Store for at least two months before eating. To add a richer flavour, prick the cake with a skewer and spoon over a couple of extra tablespoons of rum or brandy, if using, before wrapping and storing.

CLASSIC FAVOURITES

CINNAMON SWIRL CAKE

Serves: 12

Prep: 35 mins, plus cooling

Cook: 1 hour 5 mins-1 hour 10 mins

Ingredients

85 g/3 oz pecan nuts

2 tsp ground cinnamon

55 g/2 oz soft light brown sugar

225 g/8 oz self-raising flour

1 tsp baking powder

175 g/6 oz butter, softened, plus extra for greasing

175 g/6 oz caster sugar

3 large eggs, beaten

4 tbsp soured cream

Glazed pecans

1 tbsp golden syrup

2 tsp granulated sugar

12 pecan nut halves

Frosting

175 g/6 oz cream cheese

1 tbsp maple syrup

115 g/4 oz icing sugar

Method

1 Preheat the oven to 180°C/350°F/Gas Mark 4. Grease a 20-cm/8-inch square cake tin and line with baking paper.

2 Place the pecans, cinnamon and soft light brown sugar in a food processor and process until finely ground. Sift the flour and baking powder into a large bowl. Add the butter, sugar, eggs and soured cream and beat with an electric hand-held mixer until smooth.

3 Spoon a third of the mixture into the prepared tin. Sprinkle over half the pecan mix. Repeat these layers, then spread the remaining cake mixture on top. Drag through a knife to create a swirled effect. Bake in the preheated oven for 45–50 minutes, or until risen and springy to the touch. Keep the oven on. Leave to cool slightly, then transfer to a wire rack to cool completely.

4 For the glazed pecans, place the syrup and sugar in a saucepan over a low heat then stir in the pecans. Spoon onto a greased baking sheet and bake for 15 minutes. Transfer to a sheet of baking paper and leave to cool completely.

5 For the frosting, place the cream cheese and maple syrup in a bowl and beat together. Beat in the icing sugar until smooth. Frost the cake, then cut into pieces and decorate with the pecans.

ICED MADEIRA CAKE

Serves: 10

Prep: 30 mins,
plus cooling & setting

Cook: 1–1¼ hours

Ingredients

175 g/6 oz butter, softened, plus extra for greasing
175 g/6 oz caster sugar
finely grated rind of 1 lemon
3 eggs, beaten
140 g/5 oz self-raising flour
115 g/4 oz plain flour
2 tbsp milk
1 tbsp lemon juice

Icing

175 g/6 oz icing sugar
2–3 tbsp lemon juice
2 tsp lemon curd, warmed

Method

1 Preheat the oven to 160°C/325°F/Gas Mark 3. Grease a 900-g/2-lb loaf tin and line with baking paper.

2 Place the butter and caster sugar in a large bowl and beat together until light and creamy. Beat in the lemon rind, then gradually beat in the eggs.

3 Sift the self-raising and plain flour into the mixture and fold in gently until thoroughly incorporated. Fold in the milk and lemon juice.

4 Spoon the mixture into the prepared tin and bake in the preheated oven for 1–1¼ hours, or until risen, golden and springy to the touch. Leave to cool slightly, then transfer to a wire rack to cool completely.

5 For the icing, sift the icing sugar into a bowl. Add the lemon juice and stir to make a smooth and thick icing. Gently spread the icing over the top of the cake. Drizzle the warmed lemon curd over the icing and drag a skewer through the icing to create a swirled effect. Leave to set.

CLASSIC FAVOURITES

LEMON POLENTA CAKE

Serves: 8

Prep: 25 mins,
plus cooling

Cook: 40–45 mins

Ingredients

200 g/7 oz butter, softened, plus extra for greasing

200 g/7 oz caster sugar

finely grated rind and juice of 1 large lemon

3 eggs, beaten

140 g/5 oz ground almonds

100 g/3½ oz quick-cook polenta

1 tsp baking powder

crème fraîche, to serve

Syrup

juice of 2 lemons

55 g/2 oz caster sugar

2 tbsp water

Method

1 Preheat the oven to 180°C/350°F/Gas Mark 4. Grease a 20-cm/8-inch round cake tin and line with baking paper.

2 Beat the butter and sugar together until light and creamy. Beat in the lemon rind, lemon juice, eggs and ground almonds. Sift in the polenta and baking powder and stir until evenly mixed.

3 Spoon the mixture into the prepared tin. Bake in the preheated oven for 30–35 minutes, or until risen, golden and springy to the touch. Leave to cool slightly in the tin.

4 To make the syrup, place the lemon juice, sugar and water in a small saucepan. Heat gently, stirring until the sugar has dissolved, then bring to the boil and simmer for 3–4 minutes, or until slightly reduced and syrupy. Transfer the cake to a wire rack then brush half of the syrup evenly over the surface. Leave to cool completely.

5 Cut the cake into slices, drizzle the extra syrup over the top and serve with crème fraîche.

CLASSIC FAVOURITES

HUMMINGBIRD CAKE

Serves: 12

Prep: 35–40 mins, plus cooling

Cook: 25–30 mins

Ingredients

375 g/13 oz plain flour

400 g/14 oz caster sugar

1 tsp bicarbonate of soda

1 tsp salt

1 tsp ground cinnamon

3 eggs, beaten

225 ml/8 fl oz vegetable oil

1½ tsp vanilla extract

225 g/8 oz canned pineapple, undrained, finely chopped

115 g/4 oz pecan nuts, chopped

300 g/10½ oz banana, sliced

lightly toasted pecan nuts, chopped, to decorate

Frosting

225 g/8 oz cream cheese, softened

115 g/4 oz butter, softened, plus extra for greasing

450 g/1 lb icing sugar

1 tsp vanilla extract

Method

1 Preheat the oven to 180°C/350°F/Gas Mark 4. Grease three 23-cm/9-inch round cake tins and line with baking paper.

2 Sift the flour, sugar, bicarbonate of soda, salt and ground cinnamon into a large bowl and stir to combine. Add the eggs and oil and stir until the dry ingredients are incorporated. Add the vanilla, pineapple, pecan nuts and banana and mix until combined.

3 Divide the mixture evenly between the prepared tins and smooth the surfaces. Bake in the preheated oven for 25–30 minutes, or until risen, golden and a cocktail stick inserted into the centre comes out clean. Leave to cool slightly, then transfer to a wire rack to cool completely.

4 To make the frosting, beat the cream cheese and butter together using an electric hand-held mixer, until smooth. Add the icing sugar and vanilla extract and whisk until light and fluffy.

5 Place one of the cakes on a serving plate, spread about a quarter of the icing over the top and then add the second cake and repeat. Add the third cake and spread the remaining icing over the top and sides of the cake. Scatter the toasted pecan nuts on top to decorate.

DEVIL'S FOOD CAKE

Serves: 10

Prep: 35–40 mins, plus cooling

Cook: 45–50 mins

Ingredients

140 g/5 oz plain chocolate, broken into pieces

100 ml/3½ fl oz milk

2 tbsp cocoa powder

140 g/5 oz butter, softened, plus extra for greasing

140 g/5 oz light muscovado sugar

3 eggs, separated

4 tbsp soured cream or crème fraîche

200 g/7 oz plain flour

1 tsp bicarbonate of soda

Frosting

140 g/5 oz plain chocolate

40 g/1½ oz cocoa powder

4 tbsp soured cream or crème fraîche

1 tbsp golden syrup

40 g/1½ oz butter

4 tbsp water

200 g/7 oz icing sugar

Method

1 Preheat the oven to 160°C/325°F/Gas Mark 3. Grease two 20-cm/8-inch sandwich tins and line with baking paper.

2 Place the chocolate, milk and cocoa in a heatproof bowl set over a saucepan of simmering water, and heat gently until melted.

3 In a large bowl, beat together the butter and muscovado sugar until light and creamy. Beat in the egg yolks, then the soured cream and the melted chocolate. Sift in the flour and bicarbonate of soda, then fold in evenly. In a clean bowl, whisk the egg whites until they hold firm peaks. Fold into the mixture lightly.

4 Divide the mixture evenly between the prepared tins and smooth the surfaces. Bake in the preheated oven for 35–40 minutes, or until risen and springy to the touch. Leave to cool slightly, then transfer to a wire rack to cool completely.

5 To make the frosting, place the chocolate, cocoa, soured cream, golden syrup, butter and water in a saucepan and heat until melted. Sift in the icing sugar, stirring until smooth and the mixture begins to thicken. Split both cakes in half horizontally. Sandwich all the cakes together with the frosting. Spread the remainder over the top and sides of the cakes.

CLASSIC FAVOURITES

MAPLE & PECAN BUNDT CAKE

Serves: 10

Prep: 30 mins,
plus cooling & setting

Cook: 45–50 mins

Ingredients

200 g/7 oz butter, softened,
plus extra for greasing

200 g/7 oz soft light
brown sugar

3 large eggs, beaten

55 g/2 oz pecan nuts,
very finely chopped

4 tbsp maple syrup

150 ml/5 fl oz soured cream

225 g/8 oz self-raising flour,
plus extra for dusting

chopped pecan nuts,
to decorate

Icing

85 g/3 oz icing sugar

1 tbsp maple syrup

1–2 tbsp lukewarm water

Method

1 Preheat the oven to 160°C/325°F/Gas Mark 3.
Grease and lightly flour a 2-litre/3½-pint
Bundt tin.

2 Put the butter and brown sugar into a large
bowl and beat together until light and creamy.
Gradually beat in the eggs, then stir in the nuts,
maple syrup and soured cream. Sift in the flour
and fold in thoroughly.

3 Spoon the mixture into the prepared tin. Bake in
the preheated oven for 45–50 minutes, or until
risen, golden and springy to the touch. Leave to
cool slightly, then transfer to a wire rack to cool
completely.

4 To make the icing, mix the icing sugar, maple
syrup and enough water to make a smooth
icing. Spoon the icing over the top of the cake,
allowing it to run down the sides. Decorate with
the chopped nuts and leave to set.

PINEAPPLE & COCONUT RING CAKE

Serves: 12

Prep: 30 mins,
plus cooling

Cook: 25 mins

Ingredients

432 g/15½ oz canned pineapple rings, drained

115 g/4 oz butter, softened, plus extra for greasing

175 g/6 oz caster sugar

2 eggs and 1 egg yolk, beaten

225 g/8 oz plain flour, plus extra for dusting

1 tsp baking powder

½ tsp bicarbonate of soda

40 g/1½ oz desiccated coconut

Frosting

175 g/6 oz cream cheese

175 g/6 oz icing sugar

Method

1 Preheat the oven to 180°C/350°F/Gas Mark 4. Grease and lightly flour a 24-cm/9½-inch ring tin. Place the pineapple rings in a blender or food processor and process briefly until just crushed.

2 Beat together the butter and caster sugar until light and creamy. Gradually beat in the eggs until combined. Sift together the flour, baking powder and bicarbonate of soda over the egg mixture and fold in. Then fold in the crushed pineapple and the coconut.

3 Spoon the mixture into the prepared tin and bake in the preheated oven for 25 minutes, or until risen, golden and springy to the touch.

4 Leave to cool slightly, then transfer to a wire rack to cool completely. To make the frosting, mix together the cream cheese and icing sugar and spread over the cooled cake.

★ Variation

If you want a stronger pineapple flavour, add 2 tablespoons of pineapple juice from the can to the frosting mixture and stir in.

CLASSIC FAVOURITES

CHOCOLATE CAKES

CHOCOLATE CHIP SPONGE CAKE

Serves: 9

Prep: 30 mins, plus cooling & setting

Cook: 45–50 mins

Ingredients

225 g/8 oz self-raising flour

½ tsp baking powder

225 g/8 oz butter, softened, plus extra for greasing

225 g/8 oz caster sugar

55 g/2 oz ground almonds

4 eggs

1 tsp vanilla extract

140 g/5 oz milk chocolate chips

55 g/2 oz milk or plain chocolate, melted, to decorate

55 g/2 oz white chocolate, melted, to decorate

Method

1 Preheat the oven to 180°C/350°F/Gas Mark 4. Grease a 23-cm/9-inch square cake tin and line with baking paper.

2 Sift the flour and baking powder into a large bowl. Add the butter, sugar, ground almonds, eggs and vanilla extract. Using an electric hand-held mixer, beat until very light and creamy. Fold in half of the chocolate chips.

3 Spoon the mixture into the prepared tin and gently smooth the surface. Scatter over the rest of the chocolate chips. Bake in the preheated oven for 40–45 minutes, or until risen, golden and springy to the touch.

4 Leave the cake to cool slightly, then transfer to a wire rack to cool completely.

5 To decorate, spoon the melted chocolates into two separate paper piping bags. Snip off the ends and drizzle the chocolates in squiggly lines over the cake. Leave to set. Cut into nine squares and serve.

★ Variation

You could also have white and dark chocolate chips for a triple chocolate chip cake.

BOSTON CREAM PIE

Serves: 8

Prep: 40 mins,
plus chilling, cooling
& standing

Cook: 35 mins

Ingredients

225 g/8 oz self-raising flour

½ tsp salt

1 tsp baking powder

115 g/4 oz butter, softened,
plus extra for greasing

200 g/7 oz caster sugar

2 eggs, beaten

175 ml/6 fl oz milk

Pastry cream

100 g/3½ oz caster sugar

2 tbsp cornflour

3 eggs, beaten

225 ml/8 fl oz double cream

225 ml/8 fl oz milk

15 g/½ oz butter

1½ tsp vanilla extract

pinch of salt

Chocolate topping

125 ml/4 fl oz double cream

1 tsp butter

115 g/4 oz plain chocolate,
broken into pieces

Method

1 To make the pastry cream, whisk the sugar, cornflour and eggs until the whisk leaves a trail when lifted. Set aside. Bring the cream, milk and butter to the boil in a small saucepan. Add the sugar mixture and boil, whisking for 1 minute, until thickened, then strain into a bowl. Cover the surface with clingfilm and chill overnight.

2 Preheat the oven to 190°C/375°F/Gas Mark 5. Grease two 20-cm/8-inch sandwich tins and line with baking paper. Sift the flour, salt and baking powder into a large bowl. Beat together the butter and sugar until light and creamy. Gradually add the eggs, mixing well after each addition. Gradually add the milk, alternating with the flour mixture, and stir to combine. Divide the mixture evenly between the prepared tins. Bake in the preheated oven for 25 minutes, or until risen, golden and springy to the touch. Leave to cool slightly, then transfer to a wire rack to cool.

3 To make the topping, bring the cream and butter to a simmer in a small saucepan, then pour into a heatproof bowl containing the chocolate. Leave to stand for 3 minutes, then whisk gently to mix. Leave to thicken. Whisk the vanilla and salt into the pastry cream, then spread it over one of the cakes. Top with the second cake, then spread with the chocolate topping.

MOCHA CAKE

Serves: 10–12

Prep: 35–40 mins, plus cooling

Cook: 30–35 mins

Ingredients

225 g/8 oz self-raising flour

1 tsp baking powder

2 tbsp cocoa powder

225 g/8 oz butter, softened, plus extra for greasing

225 g/8 oz light soft brown sugar

4 large eggs

115 g/4 oz plain chocolate, melted

2 tbsp caster sugar

3 tbsp strong black coffee

Frosting

85 g/3 oz butter, softened

250 g/9 oz mascarpone cheese

55 g/2 oz icing sugar

2 tbsp strong black coffee

cocoa powder, to dust

chocolate-coated coffee beans, to decorate

Method

1 Preheat the oven to 180°C/350°F/Gas Mark 4. Grease two 20-cm/8-inch sandwich tins and line with baking paper.

2 Sift the flour, baking powder and cocoa powder into a large bowl. Add the butter, sugar and eggs and, using an electric hand-held mixer, beat together for 3–4 minutes, or until the mixture is very light and creamy. Fold in the melted chocolate. Divide the mixture evenly between the prepared tins and smooth the surfaces. Bake in the preheated oven for 25–30 minutes, or until risen and springy to the touch.

3 Place the caster sugar and coffee in a small saucepan and heat gently for 1–2 minutes. Cool for 10 minutes. Pierce the tops of the warm cakes all over with a skewer and spoon the coffee syrup over the cakes. Leave to cool in the tins.

4 For the frosting, place the butter and mascarpone in a bowl and beat together until well blended. Beat in the icing sugar and coffee until smooth.

5 Remove the cakes from the tins and sandwich together with half of the frosting. Swirl the remaining frosting over the top of the cake. Dust with cocoa powder and decorate with chocolate-coated coffee beans.

CHOCOLATE CAKES

CHOCOLATE & PECAN TRAY BAKE

Serves: 12–15

Prep: 30 mins, plus cooling

Cook: 40–45 mins

Ingredients

250 g/9 oz plain flour

400 g/14 oz caster sugar

25 g/1 oz cocoa powder

1 tsp bicarbonate of soda

115 g/4 oz butter, plus extra for greasing

100 g/3½ oz vegetable fat

125 ml/4 fl oz buttermilk

2 eggs, beaten

1 tsp vanilla extract

Frosting

115 g/4 oz butter

25 g/1 oz cocoa powder

5 tbsp milk

450 g/1 lb icing sugar

1 tsp vanilla extract

cinnamon stick

115 g/4 oz lightly toasted pecan nuts, chopped

Method

1 Preheat the oven to 200°C/400°F/Gas Mark 6. Grease a 33 x 23-cm/13 x 9-inch baking tin and line with baking paper. Sift the flour, sugar, cocoa powder and bicarbonate of soda into a large bowl or a food mixer and stir together to combine. Set aside.

2 Place the butter, vegetable fat and 225 ml/ 8 fl oz of water in a large saucepan over a medium heat, whisking constantly until the butter has melted. Whisk in the buttermilk, eggs and vanilla extract. Pour the butter mixture over the flour mixture and mix well.

3 Spoon the mixture into the prepared baking tin and bake in the preheated oven for 25–30 minutes, or until risen and springy to the touch. Leave to cool slightly in the tin.

4 To make the frosting, put the butter, cocoa powder and milk into a small saucepan and cook over a low heat until the butter has melted. Increase the heat and bring the mixture to the boil, stirring constantly. Stir in the sugar, vanilla, cinnamon stick and pecan nuts, then whisk until the sugar has dissolved. Leave to cool then remove the cinnamon stick and spread the icing over the cake.

CHOCOLATE CAKES

WHITE CHOCOLATE COFFEE CAKE

Serves: 10

Prep: 35 mins, plus cooling & chilling

Cook: 35–40 mins

Ingredients

40 g/1½ oz butter, plus extra for greasing

85 g/3 oz white chocolate, broken into pieces

125 g/4½ oz caster sugar

4 large eggs, beaten

2 tbsp strong black coffee

1 tsp vanilla extract

125 g/4½ oz plain flour

Frosting

175 g/6 oz white chocolate, broken into pieces

85 g/3 oz butter

125 g/4½ oz crème fraîche

125 g/4½ oz icing sugar, sifted

1 tbsp coffee liqueur

Method

1 Preheat the oven to 180°C/350°F/Gas Mark 4. Grease two 20-cm/8-inch sandwich tins and line with baking paper. Place the butter and chocolate in a heatproof bowl set over a saucepan of gently simmering water until just melted. Stir to mix, then remove from the heat. Place the caster sugar, eggs, coffee and vanilla in a bowl set over a saucepan of hot water and whisk until it leaves a trail when the whisk is lifted.

2 Remove from the heat, sift in the flour and mix in lightly and evenly. Quickly stir in the butter and chocolate mixture. Divide the mixture evenly between the prepared tins and smooth the surfaces. Bake in the preheated oven for 25–30 minutes, or until risen, golden and springy to the touch. Leave to cool slightly, then transfer to a wire rack to cool completely.

3 To make the frosting, place the chocolate and butter in a heatproof bowl set over a saucepan of gently simmering water and heat gently until melted. Remove from the heat, stir in the crème fraîche, then add the icing sugar and coffee liqueur and mix. Chill the frosting until thick. Use one third of the frosting to sandwich the cakes together, then spread the rest over the cake.

CHOCOLATE CAKES

CHOCOLATE & SOUR CHERRY CAKE

Serves: 12

Prep: 35 mins, plus cooling & chilling

Cook: 50–55 mins

Ingredients

175 g/6 oz plain chocolate, broken into pieces

115 g/4 oz butter, plus extra for greasing

3 large eggs, separated

115 g/4 oz dark muscovado sugar

115 g/4 oz self-raising flour

55 g/2 oz ground almonds

85 g/3 oz dried cherries

chocolate curls, cocoa powder and fresh cherries, to decorate

Frosting

175 g/6 oz plain chocolate, broken into pieces

5 tbsp double cream

55 g/2 oz butter

1 tbsp rum

Method

1. Preheat the oven to 180°C/350°F/Gas Mark 4. Grease a 20-cm/8-inch round cake tin and line with baking paper.

2. Place the chocolate and butter in a heatproof bowl set over a saucepan of gently simmering water and stir until melted. Leave to cool for 10 minutes, stirring occasionally.

3. Place the egg yolks and sugar in a large bowl and, using an electric hand-held mixer, beat until light and creamy. Add the melted chocolate and beat until combined. Fold in the flour, ground almonds and dried cherries.

4. In a separate bowl, whisk the egg whites until soft peaks form then gently fold into the chocolate mixture. Spoon into the prepared tin. Bake in the preheated oven for 40–45 minutes, or until risen and springy to the touch. Leave to cool slightly, then transfer to a wire rack to cool completely.

5. For the frosting, place the chocolate, cream and butter in a heatproof bowl set over a saucepan of gently simmering water. Stir until melted, then beat in the rum. Leave to cool for 20 minutes, then chill in refrigerator for about 30 minutes. Spread the frosting over the top of the cake. Decorate with chocolate curls and dust lightly with cocoa powder and top with cherries.

CHOCOLATE CAKES

CHOCOLATE MARBLE CAKE

Serves: 10

Prep: 30 mins,
plus cooling & setting

Cook: 1 hour–1 hour 10 mins

Ingredients

55 g/2 oz plain chocolate, broken into pieces

1 tbsp strong black coffee

280 g/10 oz self-raising flour

1 tsp baking powder

225 g/8 oz butter, softened, plus extra for greasing

225 g/8 oz golden caster sugar

4 eggs, beaten

50 g/1¾ oz ground almonds

2 tbsp milk

1 tsp vanilla extract

Icing

115 g/4 oz plain chocolate, broken into pieces

2 tbsp butter

Method

1 Preheat the oven to 180°C/350°F/Gas Mark 4. Grease a 1.7-litre/3-pint ring tin.

2 Put the chocolate and coffee in a heatproof bowl set over a saucepan of gently simmering water and stir until melted. Leave to cool.

3 Sift the flour and baking powder into a large bowl. Add the butter, sugar, eggs, ground almonds and milk. Beat well until smooth.

4 Transfer half of the mixture to a separate bowl and stir in the vanilla extract. Stir the cooled chocolate mixture into the other half of the mixture. Place spoonfuls of the two mixtures alternately into the prepared ring tin, then drag a skewer through to create a marbled effect. Smooth the surface.

5 Bake in the preheated oven for 50–60 minutes, or until risen and springy to the touch. Leave to cool slightly, then transfer to a wire rack to cool completely.

6 To make the icing, put the chocolate, butter and 2 tablespoons of water into a heatproof bowl set over a saucepan of gently simmering water. Stir until melted. Pour over the cake, working quickly to coat the top and sides. Leave to set before serving.

CHOCOLATE CAKES

CHOCOLATE CURLS CAKE

Serves: 20

Prep: 50 mins, plus cooling, setting & chilling

Cook: 2¼ hours

Ingredients

100 g/3½ oz cocoa powder

300 ml/10 fl oz boiling water

250 g/9 oz plain chocolate, melted

200 g/7 oz butter, softened, plus extra for greasing

500 g/1 lb 2 oz light muscovado sugar

4 eggs, beaten

375 g/13 oz plain flour

¾ tsp bicarbonate of soda

4 tsp vanilla extract

6 tbsp brandy (optional)

Ganache

500 g/1 lb 2 oz plain chocolate, chopped

500 ml/18 fl oz double cream

4 tbsp icing sugar

To decorate

200 g/7 oz plain chocolate, broken into pieces

rose petals or small edible flowers (optional)

Method

1 Preheat the oven to 160°C/325°F/Gas Mark 3. Grease a 20-cm/8-inch round cake tin and line with baking paper.

2 Carefully whisk the cocoa and water in a large bowl until smooth, then stir in the chocolate until melted. In another bowl, beat together the butter and sugar until light and creamy. Beat in the eggs, flour, bicarbonate of soda and vanilla. Stir in the chocolate mixture. Spoon the mixture into the prepared tin. Bake in the preheated oven for 2 hours, or until risen and springy to the touch. Leave to cool slightly, then transfer to a wire rack to cool completely.

3 To make the chocolate curls, place the chocolate in a heatproof bowl set over a saucepan of gently simmering water and heat until melted. Spread a thin layer on a cool slab. Leave in a cool place until set but not brittle.

4 Push a wallpaper scraper or the edge of a palette knife across the chocolate so that the chocolate starts to roll into loose curls. Place the chocolate curls on a baking sheet lined with baking paper and chill in the refrigerator while you finish the cake. Slice the cake in half horizontally. Drizzle the tops of the cake halves with brandy, if using.

5 To make the ganache, place the chocolate in a bowl. Heat the cream and icing sugar in a small saucepan and pour over the chocolate. Stir until smooth and leave to cool. Use quarter of the chocolate ganache to sandwich the cake layers together and place the cake on a flat serving plate or cake stand. Spread a thin layer of ganache around the sides of the cake with a palette knife to seal in the crumbs. Chill in the refrigerator for 15 minutes. Spread the remaining ganache all over the cake in an even layer, smoothing it so it is flat or as textured as you like. Scatter the curls over the cake so the pieces fall at different angles. Scatter with rose petals or edible flowers, if using.

VEGAN CHOCOLATE & RASPBERRY CAKE

Serves: 12

Prep: 30 mins, plus cooling

Cook: 55 mins

Ingredients

vegan margarine, for greasing

300 g/10½ oz plain flour

50 g/1¾ oz cocoa powder

1 tsp baking powder

1 tsp bicarbonate of soda

½ tsp salt

300 g/10½ oz granulated sugar

375 ml/13 fl oz soya milk

125 ml/4 fl oz rapeseed oil

7 tbsp seedless raspberry jam

1 tsp vanilla extract

fresh raspberries, to decorate

Icing

40 ml/1½ fl oz soya milk

85 g/3 oz vegan dark chocolate, broken into small pieces

60 g/2¼ oz icing sugar

1 tbsp maple syrup

Method

1 Preheat the oven to 180°C/350°F/Gas Mark 4. Grease a 23-cm/9-inch round cake tin and line with baking paper.

2 Sift the flour, cocoa, baking powder and bicarbonate of soda into a large bowl and stir in the salt and sugar. Pour the soya milk into a medium saucepan and add the oil, raspberry jam and vanilla extract. Place over a medium heat and whisk to combine. Stir into the dry ingredients and mix thoroughly.

3 Spoon the mixture into the prepared tin and bake in the preheated oven for 45 minutes, or until risen and springy to the touch. Leave to cool slightly, then transfer to a wire rack to cool completely.

4 To make the icing, heat the soya milk in a small saucepan over a medium heat until it reaches boiling point, then add the chocolate to the pan and stir until completely melted. Remove from the heat and whisk in the icing sugar and maple syrup. Set aside to cool before icing the cake, using a palette knife. Top with a few fresh raspberries before slicing and serving.

CHOCOLATE GANACHE CAKE

Serves: 10

Prep: 40 mins, plus cooling, chilling & setting

Cook: 55 mins

Ingredients

175 g/6 oz butter, plus extra for greasing

175 g/6 oz caster sugar

4 eggs, lightly beaten

250 g/9 oz self-raising flour

1 tbsp cocoa powder

50 g/1¾ oz plain chocolate, melted

200 g/7 oz chocolate-flavoured cake covering

Ganache

450 ml/16 fl oz double cream

375 g/13 oz plain chocolate, broken into pieces

Method

1 Preheat the oven to 180°C/350°F/Gas Mark 4. Grease a 20-cm/8-inch round cake tin and line with baking paper.

2 Beat the butter and sugar until light and creamy. Gradually add the eggs, beating well after each addition. Sift the flour and cocoa powder together. Fold into the cake mixture. Fold in the melted chocolate. Spoon the mixture into the prepared tin. Bake in the preheated oven for 40 minutes, or until risen and springy to the touch. Leave to cool slightly, then transfer to a wire rack to cool completely. Cut into two layers.

3 To make the ganache, place the cream in a saucepan and bring to the boil, stirring. Add the chocolate and stir until melted. Spoon into a bowl, leave to cool, then chill for 2 hours, or until set and firm. Whisk the mixture until light and fluffy. Reserve one third of the ganache. Use the remaining ganache to sandwich the cake together and spread over the top and sides. Melt the cake covering and spread it over a large sheet of baking paper. Leave to cool until just set. Cut into strips a little wider than the height. Place the strips around the edge of the cake, overlapping them slightly. Pipe the reserved ganache onto the cake.

CHOCOLATE CAKES

CHOCOLATE & PEAR CAKE

Serves: 8

Prep: 35 mins, plus cooling

Cook: 40–45 mins

Ingredients

75 g/2¾ oz butter, plus extra for greasing

2 Conference pears, peeled, cored and quartered

1 tbsp lemon juice

2 large eggs

115 g/4 oz caster sugar

½ tsp vanilla extract

90 g/3¼ oz plain flour

4 tbsp cocoa powder

¾ tsp baking powder

75 g/2¾ oz blanched hazelnuts, chopped and toasted

icing sugar, to decorate

mascarpone cheese, to serve (optional)

Method

1 Preheat the oven to 180°C/350°F/Gas Mark 4. Grease a 20-cm/8-inch round cake tin and line with baking paper.

2 Melt the butter in a small saucepan, then set aside. Brush the pear quarters with lemon juice and set aside.

3 Put the eggs and sugar into a large bowl and beat with an electric hand-held mixer for 4–5 minutes, until light and creamy, but thick enough to leave a trail when the whisk is lifted. Beat in the vanilla extract.

4 Sift in the flour, cocoa powder and baking powder. Lightly and quickly fold in the flour mixture using a large metal spoon. Slowly drizzle the melted butter around the edge of the bowl and gently fold it in, then fold in the hazelnuts.

5 Spoon the mixture into the prepared tin. Arrange the pears, cored side down, in a spoked wheel pattern. Bake in the preheated oven for 35–40 minutes, or until risen and springy to the touch. Leave to cool slightly, then transfer to a wire rack to cool completely.

6 Just before serving, generously dust the top of the cake with icing sugar. Slice and serve with a dollop of mascarpone cheese, if using.

CHOCOLATE CAKES

LOW-FAT CHOCOLATE ROLL

Serves: 12

Prep: 40 mins, plus cooling

Cook: 8–10 mins

Ingredients

3 eggs

70 g/2½ oz caster sugar, plus extra for sprinkling

1 tbsp cocoa powder

115 g/4 oz self-raising flour

1 tbsp boiled water, cooled

Filling

225 g/8 oz cottage cheese or low-fat cream cheese

1 tbsp finely grated orange rind

1 tsp clear honey

Method

1 Preheat the oven to 220°C/425°F/Gas Mark 7. Line a 30 x 23-cm/12 x 9-inch Swiss roll tin with baking paper. Cut two more sheets of the same size and reserve.

2 Break the eggs into a heatproof bowl and add the sugar. Place the bowl over a saucepan of gently simmering water and beat until the whisk leaves a trail when dragged across the surface. Remove from the heat and whisk until cool.

3 Sift the cocoa powder and flour together in a separate bowl, then stir very lightly into the egg mixture. Add the cooled boiled water, stir lightly then spoon into the prepared tin. Tap the tin on the work surface to remove any air bubbles.

4 Bake in the preheated oven for 8–10 minutes, or until springy to the touch. Invert the cake onto one of the reserved sheets of baking paper, sprinkled with caster sugar. Remove the tin and carefully strip off the baking paper. Place the other reserved sheet of baking paper on top then carefully roll up and leave until cold.

5 To make the filling, beat the cheese, orange rind and honey together in a bowl. When the Swiss roll is cool, unroll and spread with the cottage cheese mixture, then carefully roll up. Trim the edges and serve cut into thin slices.

CHOCOLATE CAKES

LOW-FAT CHOCOLATE MARBLE CAKE

Serves: 8

Prep: 35–40 mins, plus cooling

Cook: 45 mins

Ingredients

sunflower oil, for greasing

100 g/3½ oz plain flour, plus extra for dusting

3 tbsp cocoa powder

225 g/8 oz caster sugar

pinch of salt

10 egg whites

1 tsp cream of tartar

½ tsp almond extract

½ tsp vanilla extract

icing sugar, for dusting

Method

1 Preheat the oven to 180°C/350°F/Gas Mark 4. Grease and dust a 20-cm/8-inch round cake tin.

2 Sift 40 g/1½ oz of the flour with the cocoa powder and 2 tablespoons of the sugar into a bowl. Sift this mixture again three times. Sift the remaining flour with 2 tablespoons of the sugar and the salt into a separate bowl. Sift this mixture again three times.

3 Beat the egg whites into a clean, grease-free bowl until soft peaks form. Add the cream of tartar and beat in the remaining caster sugar, 1 tablespoonful at a time, until the egg whites form stiff peaks. Whisk in the almond and vanilla extract. Divide the mixture in half. Fold the cocoa and flour mixture into one half and the unflavoured flour into the other half. Spoon the cocoa-flavoured mixture into the prepared tin and top with the unflavoured mixture. Run a round-bladed knife through both mixtures to create a marbled effect.

4 Bake in the preheated oven for 45 minutes, or until risen and springy to the touch. Leave to cool slightly, then transfer to a wire rack to cool completely. Dust with icing sugar, before serving.

CHOCOLATE CAKES

CHOCOLATE & BANANA CAKE

Serves: 10–12

Prep: 30 mins, plus cooling & setting

Cook: 50–60 mins

Ingredients

1 tsp sunflower oil, for greasing

2 ripe bananas (about 225 g/8 oz in weight after peeling)

2 tbsp lemon juice

175 g/6 oz butter or margarine, softened

175 g/6 oz light muscovado sugar

2 eggs, beaten

225 g/8 oz self-raising flour

85 g/3 oz pecan nuts, roughly chopped, plus extra to decorate

55 g/2 oz plain chocolate, broken into pieces

75 g/2¾ oz white chocolate, broken into pieces

Method

1 Preheat the oven to 180°C/350°F/Gas Mark 4. Grease a 900-g/2-lb loaf tin and line with baking paper.

2 Cut the bananas into pieces, add the lemon juice and mash to form a purée. Set aside.

3 Beat the butter with the sugar in a large bowl until light and creamy. Gradually beat in the eggs, adding a little flour after each addition. When all the eggs have been added, stir in the banana purée and then the remaining flour. Add the chopped pecan nuts. Melt the plain chocolate in a heatproof bowl set over a saucepan of gently simmering water. Stir until smooth, then stir lightly into the cake mixture.

4 Spoon the mixture into the prepared tin and bake in the preheated oven for 45–55 minutes, or until risen, golden and springy to the touch. Leave to cool slightly, then transfer to a wire rack to cool completely.

5 Melt the white chocolate in a heatproof bowl set over a saucepan of gently simmering water. Stir until smooth, then drizzle over the cooled cake. Arrange the pecan nuts on top and serve once the chocolate has set.

CHOCOLATE CAKES

CHOCOLATE & ORANGE RING CAKE

Serves: 8–10

Prep: 40 mins,
plus cooling & setting

Cook: 45 mins

Ingredients

2 small oranges

250 g/9 oz self-raising flour

1½ tsp baking powder

175 g/6 oz butter, softened,
plus extra for greasing

200 g/7 oz caster sugar

3 eggs

85 g/3 oz plain chocolate,
roughly grated

Topping

175 g/6 oz icing sugar

2 tbsp orange juice

55 g/2 oz plain chocolate,
broken into pieces

Method

1 Preheat the oven to 160°C/325°F/Gas Mark 3. Grease an 850-ml/1½-pint fluted or plain ring tin.

2 Grate the rind from one of the oranges and set aside. Pare the rind from the other orange and set aside. Cut the skin and pith from the oranges, then cut them into segments by cutting down between the membranes with a sharp knife. Chop the segments into small pieces, reserving as much juice as possible.

3 Sift the flour and baking powder into a large bowl. Add the butter, caster sugar, eggs, grated orange rind and any reserved juice. Beat with an electric hand-held mixer until smooth. Fold in the chopped oranges and grated chocolate. Spoon the mixture into the prepared tin and bake in the preheated oven for 40 minutes, or until risen and springy to the touch. Leave to cool slightly, then transfer to a wire rack to cool completely.

4 Sift the icing sugar into a bowl and stir in enough orange juice to make a coating consistency. Using a spoon, drizzle the icing over the cake. Put the chocolate in a heatproof bowl set over a saucepan of gently simmering water until melted. Drizzle the chocolate over the cake. Cut the reserved orange rind into thin strips and scatter over the cake. Leave to set.

CHOCOLATE CAKES

FROSTED CHOCOLATE & CINNAMON CAKE

Serves: 16

Prep: 30 mins, plus cooling & setting

Cook: 45–50 mins

Ingredients

115 g/4 oz plain chocolate, broken into pieces

200 g/7 oz butter, plus extra for greasing

85 g/3 oz pecan nut halves

250 g/9 oz caster sugar

4 eggs, beaten

225 g/8 oz plain flour

2 tsp ground cinnamon

55 g/2 oz white chocolate, broken into pieces

2 tbsp milk

115 g/4 oz icing sugar

Method

1 Preheat the oven to 180°C/350°F/Gas Mark 4. Grease a 23-cm/9-inch square cake tin and line with baking paper.

2 Melt the plain chocolate and 175 g/6 oz of the butter in a heatproof bowl set over a pan of gently simmering water. Remove from the heat and allow to cool slightly.

3 Set 16 pecan halves to one side for decoration and chop the rest. Beat together the caster sugar and eggs with a whisk until thick and creamy. Then fold in the chocolate mixture, flour, cinnamon and chopped pecans.

4 Spoon the mixture into the prepared tin and bake in the preheated oven for 35–40 minutes, or until risen and springy to the touch. Leave to cool slightly, then transfer to a wire rack to cool completely.

5 Melt the remaining butter and white chocolate in a heatproof bowl, set over a pan of gently simmering water. Remove from the heat and beat in the milk and icing sugar. Spread this mixture over the cooled cake. Allow to set for 30 minutes then cut into 16 squares and top each square with a pecan half.

DARK CHOCOLATE YULE LOG

Serves: 8

Prep: 55 mins, plus cooling

Cook: 20 mins

Ingredients

butter, for greasing

150 g/5½ oz caster sugar, plus extra for sprinkling

4 eggs, separated

1 tsp almond extract

115 g/4 oz self-raising flour, plus extra for dusting

280 g/10 oz plain chocolate, broken into pieces

225 ml/8 fl oz double cream

2 tbsp rum

holly, to decorate

icing sugar, for dusting

Method

1 Preheat the oven to 190°C/375°F/Gas Mark 5. Grease a 40 x 28-cm/16 x 11-inch Swiss roll tin, then dust with flour.

2 Reserve 2 tablespoons of the caster sugar and whisk the remainder with the egg yolks in a bowl until thick and pale. Stir in the almond extract. Whisk the egg whites in a clean, grease-free bowl until soft peaks form. Gradually whisk in the reserved sugar until stiff and glossy. Sift half of the flour over the egg yolk mixture and fold in, then fold in one quarter of the egg whites. Sift and fold in the remaining flour, followed by the remaining egg whites. Spoon the mixture into the prepared tin, spreading it out evenly with a palette knife. Bake in the preheated oven for 15 minutes, or until risen and springy to the touch.

3 Sprinkle caster sugar over a sheet of baking paper and turn out the cake onto the paper. Roll up and leave to cool.

4 Place the chocolate in a heatproof bowl. Bring the cream to boiling point in a small saucepan, then pour it over the chocolate and stir until the chocolate has melted. Beat with an electric hand-held mixer until the mixture is smooth.

5 Reserve about one third of the chocolate mixture and stir the rum into the remainder. Unroll the cake and spread the chocolate-and-rum mixture over the top. Re-roll and place on a plate or silver board. Spread the reserved chocolate mixture evenly over the top and sides. Mark with a fork so that the surface resembles tree bark. Just before serving, decorate with holly and a sprinkling of icing sugar to resemble snow.

CHOCOLATE & COCONUT CAKE

Serves: 6

Prep: 35 mins,
plus cooling & setting

Cook: 45 mins

Ingredients

175 g/6 oz butter or
margarine, plus extra
for greasing

175 g/6 oz caster sugar

3 eggs, beaten

175 g/6 oz self-raising flour

2 tbsp cocoa powder

about 8 tbsp dessicated
coconut, to decorate

150 ml/5 fl oz double cream,
whipped, to decorate

Frosting

50 g/1¾ oz plain chocolate,
broken into pieces

5 tbsp milk

1 tsp butter

85 g/3 oz icing sugar

Method

1 Preheat the oven to 180°C/350°F/Gas Mark 4.
Grease a 450-g/1-lb loaf tin and line with
baking paper.

2 Beat the butter and caster sugar together in a
bowl until light and creamy. Gradually add the
eggs, beating well after each addition. Sift the
flour and cocoa together. Fold into the mixture.

3 Spoon the mixture into the prepared tin. Bake in
the preheated oven for 40 minutes, or until risen
and springy to the touch. Leave to cool slightly,
then transfer to a wire rack to cool completely.

4 To make the frosting, place the chocolate,
milk and butter in a heatproof bowl set over a
saucepan of gently simmering water. Stir until the
chocolate has melted. Add the icing sugar and
beat until smooth. Leave the frosting to cool until
it is thick enough to spread, then spread all over
the cake. Sprinkle with the desiccated coconut
and leave to stand until the icing has set.

5 Cut a V-shaped wedge from the top of the
cake. Put the cream in a piping bag fitted with
a plain or star nozzle. Pipe the cream down the
centre of the channel, then replace the wedge
of cake. Pipe cream down either side of the
wedge of cake.

CHOCOLATE CAKES

NO-BAKE CHOCOLATE REFRIGERATOR CAKE

Serves: 12

Prep: 20 mins, plus setting

Cook: 5 mins

Ingredients

225 g/8 oz plain chocolate, broken into pieces

225 g/8 oz butter

3 tbsp strong black coffee

55 g/2 oz light brown sugar

a few drops of vanilla extract

225 g/8 oz digestive biscuits, crushed

85 g/3 oz raisins

85 g/3 oz chopped walnuts

Method

1 Line a 20-cm/8-inch round cake tin with baking paper.

2 Melt the chocolate and butter with the coffee, sugar and vanilla extract in a large saucepan over a low heat.

3 Stir in the crushed biscuits, raisins and walnuts and mix well to combine.

4 Spoon the mixture into the prepared tin. Transfer to the refrigerator and leave to set for 1–2 hours.

5 Remove carefully from the tin and cut into thin slices to serve.

CHOCOLATE & ALMOND CAKE

Serves: 8–10

Prep: 25 mins, plus cooling

Cook: 1–1¼ hours

Ingredients

125 g/4½ oz butter, softened, plus extra for greasing

125 g/4½ oz caster sugar

4 tsp cocoa powder

½ tsp baking powder

4 eggs

¼ tsp vanilla extract

2 tbsp Marsala or orange juice

125 g/4½ oz plain chocolate, very finely chopped

200 g/7 oz ground almonds

icing sugar, for dusting

Method

1 Preheat the oven to 180°C/350°F/Gas Mark 4. Grease a 20-cm/8-inch round cake tin and line with baking paper.

2 Put the butter and sugar into a large bowl and beat with an electric hand-held mixer until light and creamy. Sift in the cocoa powder and baking powder and fold them in. Gradually add the eggs one at a time, beating until each is incorporated before adding the next. Stir in the vanilla extract and Marsala.

3 Add the chocolate and ground almonds and stir. Spoon the mixture into the prepared tin. Bake in the preheated oven for 1–1¼ hours, or until risen and springy to the touch.

4 Leave to cool slightly, then transfer to a wire rack to cool completely.

5 Just before serving, generously dust the top of the cake with icing sugar.

MOCHA SLAB CAKE

Serves: 12

Prep: 30 mins, plus cooling & setting

Cook: 35–40 mins

Ingredients

3 tbsp cocoa powder

1 tbsp espresso coffee powder

4 tbsp boiling water

200 g/7 oz self-raising flour

1 tsp baking powder

175 g/6 oz butter, softened, plus extra for greasing

175 g/6 oz caster sugar

3 eggs

1 tsp vanilla extract

1 tbsp milk

Frosting

200 g/7 oz mascarpone cheese

40 g/1½ oz caster sugar

1 tbsp strong coffee, cooled

4 tbsp double cream

85 g/3 oz plain chocolate, melted

Method

1 Preheat the oven to 180°C/350°F/Gas Mark 4. Grease an 18 x 28-cm/7 x 11-inch baking tin and line with baking paper.

2 Put the cocoa powder, coffee powder and boiling water in a heatproof bowl and mix together to a smooth paste. Leave to cool for 10 minutes.

3 Sift the flour and baking powder into a large bowl and add the butter, sugar, eggs, vanilla extract, milk and cocoa mixture. Beat with an electric hand-held mixer for 2–3 minutes, or until smooth.

4 Spoon the mixture into the prepared tin. Bake in the preheated oven for 30–35 minutes, or until risen and springy to the touch. Leave to cool slightly, then transfer to a wire rack to cool completely.

5 To make the frosting, put the mascarpone cheese, sugar, coffee and cream in a bowl and beat together until smooth. Spread over the top of the cake. Spoon the melted chocolate into a paper piping bag, snip off the end and pipe thin zig-zag lines across the frosting. Leave to set.

GLUTEN-FREE CHOCOLATE FUDGE CAKE

Serves: 8–10

Prep: 30 mins, plus cooling

Cook: 40 mins

Ingredients

125 g/4½ oz gluten-free plain chocolate, broken into pieces

125 g/4½ oz butter, plus extra for greasing

200 g/7 oz light soft brown sugar

100 g/3½ oz caster sugar

1 tsp glycerine

2 eggs, beaten

100 ml/3½ fl oz plain yogurt

½ tsp vanilla extract

100 g/3½ oz rice flour

100 g/3½ oz gluten-free, wheat-free self-raising flour

1 tsp xanthan gum

1½ tsp gluten-free baking powder

½ tsp gluten-free bicarbonate of soda

Frosting

150 g/5½ oz gluten-free plain chocolate, broken into pieces

150 ml/5 fl oz double cream

100 g/3½ oz butter

175 g/6 oz gluten-free icing sugar

Method

1 Preheat the oven to 180°C/350°F/Gas Mark 4. Grease two 20-cm/8-inch sandwich tins and line with baking paper.

2 Melt the chocolate in a heatproof bowl set over a pan of simmering water. In a separate bowl, cream the butter, sugars and glycerine until light and creamy. Slowly add the eggs and beat well. Add the yogurt, vanilla and the chocolate. Fold in the flours, xanthan gum, baking powder and bicarbonate of soda. Add a little warm water if the mixture is too stiff.

3 Divide the mixture evenly between the prepared tins and smooth the surfaces. Bake in the preheated oven for 30 minutes, or until risen and springy to the touch. Leave to cool slightly, then transfer to a wire rack to cool completely.

4 To make the frosting, melt the chocolate and cream in a heatproof bowl set over a pan of simmering water. Beat the butter and sugar in a separate bowl and then add the chocolate mixture. Beat until it has a fudge-like consistency.

5 Spread the top of one sponge with some of the fudge frosting and place the other sponge on top. Spread the rest of the fudge frosting over the top and sides of the cake. Refrigerate for 30 minutes before serving.

CHOCOLATE CAKES

WHITE CHOCOLATE CAKE

Serves: 12

Prep: 30 mins,
plus cooling & chilling

Cook: 35 mins

Ingredients

butter, for greasing

50 g/1¾ oz white chocolate, broken into pieces

2 eggs

50 g/1¾ oz caster sugar

70 g/2½ oz plain flour

50 g/1¾ oz white chocolate shavings, to decorate

Truffle topping

300 ml/10 fl oz double cream

350 g/12 oz white chocolate, broken into pieces

250 g/9 oz mascarpone cheese

Method

1 Preheat the oven to 180°C/350°F/Gas Mark 4. Grease a 20-cm/8-inch round cake tin and line with baking paper. Melt the white chocolate in a heatproof bowl set over a saucepan of gently simmering water.

2 Using a electric hand-held mixer, beat the eggs and sugar together in a large bowl until pale and thick – the mixture should leave a trail when the whisk is lifted. Sift in the flour and gently fold in with a metal spoon. Add the melted chocolate. Spoon the mixture into the prepared tin and bake in the preheated oven for 25 minutes, or until risen, golden and springy to the touch. Leave to cool slightly, then transfer to a wire rack to cool completely.

3 To make the topping, put the cream in a saucepan and bring to the boil, stirring constantly. Leave to cool slightly, then add the white chocolate and stir until melted and combined. Remove from the heat and set aside until almost cool, stirring, then mix in the mascarpone cheese. Pour on top of the cake. Chill in the refrigerator for 2 hours.

4 To decorate, arrange the shavings carefully on the top of the cake. Serve immediately.

CHOCOLATE CAKES

CHOCOLATE MADEIRA CAKE

Serves: 8-10

Prep: 30 mins,
plus cooling

Cook: 50-55 mins

Ingredients

1 tsp sunflower oil,
for greasing

55 g/2 oz self-raising flour

1 tsp baking powder

115 g/4 oz butter or
margarine, softened

115 g/4 oz caster sugar

3 eggs, beaten

25 g/1 oz ground almonds

115 g/4 oz drinking
chocolate powder

icing sugar, for dusting

Icing

225 g/8 oz icing sugar

1½ tbsp cocoa powder

2 tbsp butter

3-4 tbsp hot water

Method

1 Preheat the oven to 180°C/350°F/Gas Mark 4.
Grease an 18-cm/7-inch round cake tin and
line with baking paper. Sift the flour and baking
powder together and set aside.

2 Beat the butter with the sugar until light and
creamy, then gradually beat in the eggs, adding
a little of the flour after each addition. When all
the eggs have been added, stir in the remaining
flour together with the ground almonds. Sift the
drinking chocolate powder into the mixture and
stir lightly.

3 Spoon the mixture into the prepared tin. Bake
in the preheated oven for 50–55 minutes, or
until risen and springy to the touch. Leave to
cool slightly, then transfer to a wire rack to cool
completely.

4 To make the icing, sift the icing sugar and cocoa
together into a large bowl and make a hollow
in the centre. Place the butter in the centre.
Mix with sufficient hot water to form a smooth
spreadable icing. Coat the top and sides of the
cake with icing, swirling it to give a decorative
effect. Dust with icing sugar.

CHOCOLATE CAKES

CHOCOLATE SACHERTORTE CAKE

Serves: 10

Prep: 45 mins,
plus cooling & setting

Cook: 1 hour 20 mins–
1 hour 35 mins

Ingredients

175 g/6 oz plain chocolate, broken into pieces

140 g/5 oz butter, softened, plus extra for greasing

140 g/5 oz caster sugar

6 eggs, separated

175 g/6 oz plain flour

6 tbsp apricot jam, warmed

Icing

225 g/8 oz plain chocolate, broken into pieces

5 tbsp strong black coffee

115 g/4 oz icing sugar

Method

1 Preheat the oven to 150°C/300°F/Gas Mark 2. Grease a 23-cm/9-inch round cake tin and line with baking paper.

2 Melt the chocolate in a heatproof bowl set over a saucepan of gently simmering water. Beat the butter and 70 g/2½ oz of the caster sugar in a large bowl until light and creamy. Add the egg yolks and beat well. Add the melted chocolate in a thin stream, beating well. Sift the flour, then fold into the mixture. Whisk the egg whites in a clean, grease-free bowl until soft peaks form. Add the remaining caster sugar and whisk until stiff and glossy. Fold half of the egg whites into the chocolate mixture, then fold in the remainder.

3 Spoon the mixture into the prepared tin. Bake in the preheated oven for 1–1¼ hours, or until risen and springy to the touch. Leave to cool slightly, then transfer to a wire rack to cool completely.

4 To make the icing, melt 175 g/6 oz of the chocolate in a heatproof bowl set over a saucepan of gently simmering water. Beat in the coffee. Whisk this mixture into the icing sugar in a bowl to form a thick icing.

CHOCOLATE CAKES

5 Cut the cake horizontally in half. Sandwich the layers together with the jam. Place back on the wire rack. Spoon over the icing and spread to coat the top and sides. Leave to set for 5 minutes, letting any excess drip through the rack. Transfer to a serving plate and leave to set for at least 2 hours.

6 Melt the remaining chocolate in a heatproof bowl set over gently simmering water and spoon into a piping bag fitted with a fine plain nozzle. Pipe 'Sachertorte' on the cake top and leave to set.

CHOCOLATE SWIRL LOAF

Serves: 8

Prep: 35 mins,
plus chilling, rising & cooling

Cook: 50–55 mins

Ingredients

6 egg yolks

175 g/6 oz butter, melted, plus extra for greasing

1 tsp vanilla extract

100 g/3½ oz caster sugar

½ tsp salt

250 ml/9 fl oz milk

5 tsp easy-blend dried yeast

475 g/1 lb 1 oz plain flour, plus extra for dusting

icing sugar, for dusting

Chocolate filling

225 g/8 oz plain chocolate, at least 70 per cent cocoa solids, roughly chopped

1 tbsp cocoa powder

½ tsp ground cinnamon

100 g/3½ oz caster sugar

100 g/3½ oz walnuts, roughly chopped

Method

1 Whisk the egg yolks in a bowl, then gradually add the butter and vanilla extract. Add the sugar and salt and stir to combine. Heat the milk in a small saucepan until lukewarm. Add the yeast and stir to dissolve. Sift the flour into a large bowl, then pour in the egg mixture and milk, stirring constantly. Mix until a smooth, elastic dough forms. Transfer to a bowl, cover with clingfilm and chill in the refrigerator for 1½ hours.

2 To make the filling, put the chocolate, cocoa powder and cinnamon into a food processor and process until fine crumbs form. Combine the chocolate mixture with the sugar.

3 Grease a 25-cm/10-inch loaf tin and line a baking tray with baking paper. Turn out the dough onto a lightly floured work surface, then roll out to a 25-cm/10-inch square and place on the prepared tray. Spread the chocolate mixture evenly on the dough and top with the walnuts, then fold the dough over slightly at two opposite sides of the square and press down. Place in the prepared tin, with the joins at the base, cover with a damp tea towel and let rise for 1 hour. Preheat the oven to 180°C/350°F/Gas Mark 4.

4 Bake in the preheated oven for 40–45 minutes, or until risen and golden. Transfer to a wire rack to cool completely, then dust with icing sugar.

CHOCOLATE CAKES

CHOCOLATE BROWNIE CAKE

Serves: 10

Prep: 30–35 mins,
plus cooling & setting

Cook: 35–40 mins

Ingredients

200 g/7 oz butter,
plus extra for greasing

115 g/4 oz plain chocolate,
broken into pieces

280 g/10 oz granulated
sugar

115 g/4 oz light muscovado
sugar

4 eggs, beaten

175 g/6 oz plain flour

1 tsp vanilla extract

pinch of salt

75 g/2¾ oz dried
cranberries

75 g/2¾ oz toasted flaked
almonds, plus extra to
decorate

Frosting

115 g/4 oz plain chocolate,
broken into pieces

25 g/1 oz butter

225 g/8 oz icing sugar

3–4 tbsp milk

Method

1 Preheat the oven to 180°C/350°F/Gas Mark 4.
Grease two 20-cm/8-inch sandwich tins and line
with baking paper.

2 Place the butter in a saucepan and add the
chocolate. Heat gently, stirring frequently until
the mixture has melted. Remove from the heat
and stir until smooth. Add the sugars, stir well,
then leave to cool for 10 minutes.

3 Gradually add the eggs to the chocolate
mixture, beating well after each addition. Stir in
the flour, vanilla and salt. Stir in the cranberries
and flaked almonds. Divide the mixture between
the prepared tins and smooth the surfaces.

4 Bake in the preheated oven for 25–30 minutes,
or until risen and springy to the touch. Leave to
cool slightly, then transfer to a wire rack to cool
completely.

5 To make the frosting, melt the chocolate and
butter in a saucepan and stir until smooth.
Gradually beat in the icing sugar with enough
milk to give a smooth consistency. Use a little
of the frosting to sandwich the two cakes
together, then spread the top and sides with the
remainder, swirling the top to give a decorative
effect. Sprinkle the flaked almonds over the top
to decorate. Leave to set.

CHOCOLATE CAKES

CHOCOLATE & WALNUT CAKE

Serves: 8

Prep: 35 mins, plus cooling

Cook: 40–45 mins

Ingredients

4 eggs

125 g/4½ oz caster sugar

75 g/2¾ oz plain chocolate, broken into pieces

125 g/4½ oz plain flour

1 tbsp cocoa powder

25 g/1 oz butter, melted, plus extra for greasing

115 g/4 oz walnuts, finely chopped

walnut halves, to decorate

Frosting

75 g/2¾ oz plain chocolate, broken into pieces

115 g/4 oz butter, softened

175 g/6 oz icing sugar

2 tbsp milk

Method

1 Preheat the oven to 160°C/325°F/Gas Mark 3. Grease an 18-cm/7-inch round cake tin and line with baking paper.

2 Place the eggs and caster sugar in a bowl and beat with an electric hand-held mixer for 10 minutes, or until a trail is left when the whisk is dragged across the surface. Put the chocolate in a heatproof bowl set over a saucepan of gently simmering water until melted.

3 Sift the flour and cocoa and fold into the egg mixture with a spoon. Fold in the butter, melted chocolate and walnuts. Spoon into the prepared tin and bake for 30–35 minutes, or until risen and springy to the touch. Leave to cool slightly, then transfer to a wire rack to cool completely.

4 To make the frosting, melt the chocolate and leave to cool. Beat the butter, icing sugar and milk until pale. Whisk in the chocolate. Cut the cake in half horizontally. Spread one cake half with frosting and put the other cake half on top. Spread the remaining frosting over the top. Decorate with walnut halves.

★ **Variation**

For a creamier, sweeter cake, use milk chocolate for the frosting.

CHOCOLATE CAKES

FRUIT & NUT CAKES

APPLE CRUMB CAKE

Serves: 10

Prep: 30 mins, plus cooling

Cook: 1 hour 10 mins– 1 hour 20 mins

Ingredients

175 g/6 oz butter, softened, plus extra for greasing

175 g/6 oz caster sugar

3 large eggs, beaten

2 tbsp milk

225 g/8 oz self-raising flour

1 tsp ground cinnamon

½ tsp grated nutmeg

2 cooking apples, peeled, cored and chopped (500 g/1 lb 2 oz unpeeled weight)

clotted cream, to serve (optional)

Crumb topping

85 g/3 oz self-raising flour

55 g/2 oz butter, chilled and diced

55 g/2 oz demerara sugar

55 g/2 oz blanched hazelnuts, chopped

Method

1 Preheat the oven to 180°C/350°F/Gas Mark 4. Grease a 23-cm/9-inch round cake tin and line with baking paper.

2 Put the butter and caster sugar into a large bowl and beat together until light and creamy, then gradually beat in the eggs. Stir in the milk. Sift together the flour and spices and gently fold in. Spoon half the mixture into the prepared tin and scatter over half the apples. Spoon over the remaining mixture and spread evenly. Top with the remaining apples.

3 To make the topping, sift the flour into a bowl, then add the butter and rub in until the mixture resembles breadcrumbs. Stir in the sugar and nuts. Sprinkle the mixture evenly over the cake.

4 Bake in the preheated oven for 1 hour, then cover loosely with foil to prevent over-browning. Cook for a further 10–20 minutes, or until risen, golden and springy to the touch. Leave to cool slightly, then transfer to a wire rack to cool completely. Serve warm or cold, with clotted cream, if using.

★ Variation

For a smoother topping, you could use ground almonds instead of the chopped hazelnuts.

FRUIT & NUT CAKES

CINNAMON & WALNUT LAYER CAKE

Serves: 10

Prep: 40–45 mins, **Cook: 20–25 mins**
plus cooling

Ingredients

250 g/9 oz soft light brown sugar

250 g/9 oz plain flour

2 tsp ground cinnamon, plus extra for dusting

1 tsp bicarbonate of soda

3 eggs, beaten

200 ml/7 fl oz sunflower oil, plus extra for greasing

125 g/4½ oz walnuts, finely chopped

1 large ripe banana (about 175 g/6 oz unpeeled weight), mashed

walnut pieces, to decorate

Frosting

175 g/6 oz cream cheese

225 g/8 oz butter, softened

1 tsp ground cinnamon

225 g/8 oz icing sugar

Method

1 Preheat the oven to 180°C/350°F/Gas Mark 4. Grease three 20-cm/8-inch sandwich tins and line with baking paper.

2 Put the brown sugar into a large bowl and sift in the flour, cinnamon and bicarbonate of soda. Add the eggs, oil, walnuts and banana and beat with a wooden spoon until thoroughly mixed.

3 Divide the mixture evenly between the prepared tins and smooth the surfaces. Bake in the preheated oven for 20–25 minutes, or until risen and springy to the touch. Leave to cool slightly, then transfer to wire racks to cool completely.

4 To make the frosting, put the cheese, butter and cinnamon into a bowl and beat together until smooth and creamy. Stir in the icing sugar and mix until smooth.

5 Sandwich the three cakes together with one third of the frosting and spread the remainder over the top and sides of the cake. Decorate with the walnut pieces and a dusting of cinnamon.

ORANGE MADEIRA RING CAKE

Serves: 8

Prep: 30 mins, plus cooling

Cook: 45–55 mins

Ingredients

1 tbsp golden syrup (plus extra for drizzling, if liked)

2 medium oranges, peeled and sliced

175 g/6 oz butter, plus extra for greasing

175 g/6 oz caster sugar

3 eggs, beaten

115 g/4 oz plain flour

115 g/4 oz self-raising flour

finely grated rind of 1 orange

2–3 tbsp orange juice

Method

1 Preheat the oven to 160°C/325°F/Gas Mark 3. Grease a 1.5-litre/2¾-pint ring cake tin and spoon the syrup into the base. Arrange the orange slices over the syrup in the tin.

2 Beat together the butter and sugar until light and creamy. Gradually beat in the eggs, beating well after each addition.

3 Sift the flours into the mixture and fold in, adding the orange rind and enough juice to make a soft consistency.

4 Spoon the mixture into the prepared tin. Bake in the preheated oven for 45–55 minutes, or until risen, golden and springy to the touch. Leave to cool slightly, then transfer to a wire rack to cool completely.

FRUIT & NUT CAKES

PEAR & PECAN SPONGE CAKE

Serves: 8

Prep: 30 mins,
plus cooling

Cook: 40–45 mins

Ingredients

1 large egg, beaten

100 g/3½ oz light
muscovado sugar

3 tbsp golden syrup

3 tbsp milk

3 tbsp sunflower oil

125 g/4½ oz self-raising flour

1 tsp ground ginger

1 tsp ground cinnamon

Greek-style yogurt or
custard, to serve

Topping

15 g/½ oz butter, plus extra
for greasing

1 tbsp golden syrup

4 ripe pears

4 pecan nuts, halved

Method

1 Preheat the oven to 180°C/350°F/Gas Mark 4.
Grease a 22-cm/8½-inch round cake tin and line
with baking paper.

2 To make the topping, put the butter and
golden syrup into a saucepan and heat gently,
stirring, until melted. Pour into the prepared tin,
spreading to cover the base.

3 Thinly peel the pears, cut in half lengthways and
use a teaspoon to scoop out the cores. Place a
pecan half in the cavity of each pear half and
arrange cut-side down in the tin.

4 Place the egg, sugar, golden syrup, milk and oil
into a large bowl and beat together. Sift together
the flour, ginger and cinnamon and stir into the
egg mixture. Beat well until smooth.

5 Spoon the mixture over the pears in the tin. Bake
in the preheated oven for 35–40 minutes, or until
risen, golden and springy to the touch.

6 Leave to cool slightly, then turn out onto a
serving plate and serve with yogurt.

FRUIT & NUT CAKES

BLUEBERRY TRAY BAKE

Serves: 12

Prep: 30–35 mins, plus cooling **Cook: 40 mins**

Ingredients

250 g/9 oz plain flour, plus extra for dusting

1 tsp baking powder

175 g/6 oz butter, softened, plus extra for greasing

85 g/3 oz caster sugar

1 egg, beaten

Topping

2 eggs

150 ml/5 fl oz whipping cream

55 g/2 oz caster sugar

4 tbsp blueberry jam

200 g/7 oz fresh blueberries

Method

1 Preheat the oven to 180°C/350°F/Gas Mark 4. Grease a 23 x 33-cm/9 x 13-inch Swiss roll tin and line with baking paper.

2 Sift the flour and baking powder into a large bowl and add the butter. Rub the butter into the flour until it resembles coarse breadcrumbs. Stir in the sugar and egg and beat until the mixture starts to clump together.

3 Gather the mixture together and knead lightly on a floured surface. Press the mixture out in an even layer in the base of the prepared tin, using floured hands. Prick the mixture all over with the prongs of a fork.

4 Bake in the preheated oven for 15 minutes, or until golden and springy to the touch. Leave to cool slightly in the tin and keep the oven on.

5 To make the topping, place the eggs, cream and sugar in a bowl and whisk until smooth.

6 Spread the jam over the part-baked base, then gently spoon over the egg mixture. Scatter over the blueberries and return to the oven for 25 minutes, or until the topping is set and the cake is golden. Cut into slices and serve either warm or cold.

CHERRY MARBLE CAKE

Serves: 12

Prep: 35 mins, plus cooling

Cook: 1 hour

Ingredients

2 tbsp dried breadcrumbs

250 g/9 oz butter, softened, plus extra for greasing

250 g/9 oz caster sugar

4 eggs, beaten

500 g/1 lb 2 oz plain flour

2 tsp baking powder

½ tsp salt

100 ml/3½ fl oz milk

300 g/10½ oz fresh cherries, stoned

30 g/1 oz cocoa powder

icing sugar, for dusting

Method

1 Preheat the oven to 180°C/350°F/Gas Mark 4. Grease a 26-cm/10½-inch deep Bundt tin and sprinkle with the breadcrumbs.

2 Put the butter and sugar into a bowl and beat until light and creamy. Gradually add the eggs, beating after each addition until smooth.

3 Sift the flour with the baking powder and salt into a large bowl. Gradually add the flour mixture to the butter mixture, alternating with the milk and beating until the mixture is thick and smooth.

4 Spoon half of the mixture into the prepared tin. Scatter half of the cherries over the cake mixture, pressing them in slightly. Stir the cocoa powder into the remaining cake mixture.

5 Spoon the cocoa mixture over the cherries, then scatter the remaining cherries on top. Using the handle of a wooden spoon, gently swirl the two layers together to produce a marbled effect.

6 Bake in the preheated oven for about 1 hour, or until risen, golden and springy to the touch. Leave to cool slightly, then transfer to a wire rack to cool completely. Dust with icing sugar just before serving.

FRUIT & NUT CAKES

PEAR & GINGER CAKE

Serves: 8–10

Prep: 30 mins,
plus cooling

Cook: 35–40 mins

Ingredients

200 g/7 oz butter, softened, plus extra for greasing
200 g/7 oz caster sugar
200 g/7 oz self-raising flour
1 tbsp ground ginger
3 eggs
450 g/1 lb pears, peeled, cored and thinly sliced
1 tbsp soft light brown sugar

Method

1 Preheat the oven to 180°C/350°F/Gas Mark 4. Grease a 20-cm/8-inch deep round cake tin and line with baking paper.

2 Put 175 g/6 oz of the butter and the caster sugar into a large bowl. Sift in the flour and ground ginger and add the eggs. Beat well with an electric hand-held mixer until smooth.

3 Spoon the mixture into the prepared tin, smoothing the surface with a palette knife. Arrange the pear slices over the cake mixture. Sprinkle with the brown sugar and dot with the remaining butter.

4 Bake in the preheated oven for 35–40 minutes, or until risen, golden and springy to the touch.

5 Leave to cool slightly, then transfer to a wire rack to cool completely.

FRUIT & NUT CAKES

PINEAPPLE UPSIDE-DOWN CAKE

Serves: 6

Prep: 30–35 mins, plus cooling

Cook: 50–55 mins

Ingredients

115 g/4 oz butter

225 g/8 oz soft light brown sugar

550 g/1 lb 4 oz canned pineapple rings, plus 4 tbsp juice from can

7 maraschino cherries

12 pecan nut halves

3 egg yolks

200 g/7 oz caster sugar

115 g/4 oz plain flour

1 tsp baking powder

½ tsp salt

1 tsp vanilla extract

2 egg whites

Method

1. Preheat the oven to 180°C/350°F/Gas Mark 4. Melt the butter in an ovenproof 25-cm/10-inch casserole dish over a low heat. Scatter the brown sugar into the dish and remove it from the heat.

2. Arrange 7 pineapple rings over the sugar mixture in the dish. Cut the remaining pineapple rings in half horizontally and use to line the sides of the dish. Place a cherry in the centre of each ring, then arrange the pecan halves between the rings.

3. Beat the egg yolks using an electric hand-held mixer until thick and a lemony colour. Gradually add the caster sugar, beating well. In a separate bowl, sift in the flour, baking powder and salt and stir. Add the dry ingredients to the egg mixture, alternating it with the pineapple juice, mixing well. Stir in the vanilla extract.

4. Beat the egg whites in a clean, grease-free bowl, using an electric hand-held mixer, until they form stiff peaks. Fold the beaten egg whites into the cake mixture. Spoon the mixture evenly over the pineapples in the dish. Bake in the preheated oven for 45–50 minutes, or until the cake is set. Leave to cool slightly, before turning the cake out on to a serving plate.

FRUIT & NUT CAKES

BANANA & COCONUT LOAF

Serves: 10   **Prep: 20 mins,** plus cooling   **Cook: 1 hour**

Ingredients

250 g/9 oz plain flour

1½ tsp baking powder

200 g/7 oz caster sugar

55 g/2 oz desiccated coconut

2 eggs, beaten

90 ml/3 fl oz sunflower oil, plus extra for greasing

2 ripe bananas, mashed

125 ml/4 fl oz soured cream

1 tsp vanilla extract

long shreds of coconut, toasted, to decorate

Method

1 Preheat the oven to 180°C/350°F/Gas Mark 4. Grease a 450-g/1-lb loaf tin and line with baking paper.

2 Sift together the flour and baking powder in a large bowl. Stir in the sugar and coconut. Beat together the eggs, oil, bananas, cream and vanilla extract in a large bowl. Stir into the dry ingredients, mixing until evenly combined.

3 Spoon the mixture into the prepared tin. Bake in the preheated oven for about 1 hour, or until risen, golden and springy to the touch.

4 Leave to cool slightly, then transfer to a wire rack to cool completely. Decorate with shreds of coconut.

PISTACHIO ANGEL CAKE

Serves: 8

Prep: 25 mins, plus cooling

Cook: 25–30 mins

Ingredients

sunflower oil, for greasing

6 egg whites

¾ tsp cream of tartar

175 g/6 oz caster sugar

1 tsp vanilla extract

40 g/1½ oz pistachio nuts, finely chopped

85 g/3 oz rice flour, plus extra for dusting

fresh fruit, to serve

Method

1 Preheat the oven to 160°C/325°F/Gas Mark 3. Grease a 1.5-litre/2¾-pint ring tin and dust lightly with a little flour, tipping out the excess.

2 Whisk the egg whites with an electric hand-held mixer in a clean, grease-free bowl until they hold soft peaks. Stir the cream of tartar into the sugar in a small bowl, then gradually whisk into the egg whites, whisking at high speed until the mixture holds stiff peaks. Whisk in the vanilla.

3 In a separate small bowl, stir the pistachios into the flour. Fold the pistachio mixture into the egg white mixture lightly and evenly using a large metal spoon.

4 Spoon the mixture into the prepared tin and tap the tin to remove any large air bubbles. Bake in the preheated oven for 25–30 minutes, or until risen, golden and springy to the touch.

5 Invert the cake onto a wire rack and leave to cool upside down in the tin. When cool, run the tip of a knife around the edges of the cake to loosen, then turn out onto a plate and serve with fresh fruit.

GLUTEN-FREE CARROT CAKE

Serves: 10

Prep: 30 mins, plus cooling

Cook: 1 hour 20 mins

Ingredients

butter, for greasing

250 ml/9 fl oz vegetable oil

290 g/10¼ oz soft light brown sugar

3 eggs

10 g/¼ oz ground almonds

450 g/1 lb carrots, coarsely grated

115 g/4 oz chopped walnuts

375 g/13 oz gluten-free, wheat-free self-raising flour

1 tsp gluten-free bicarbonate of soda

1½ tsp ground mixed spice

walnut halves, to decorate (optional)

Frosting

60 g/2¼ oz butter, softened

160 g/5¾ oz gluten-free cream cheese

zest of 1 lemon and juice of ½ lemon

500 g/1 lb 2 oz gluten-free icing sugar

Method

1 Preheat the oven to 180°C/350°F/Gas Mark 4. Grease a 20-cm/8-inch round cake tin and line with baking paper.

2 In a large bowl, beat the oil, sugar and eggs with an electric hand-held mixer until fluffy. Slowly fold in the rest of the cake ingredients.

3 Spoon the mixture into the prepared tin and bake in the preheated oven for 1 hour 20 minutes, or until risen and springy to the touch.

4 Leave to cool slightly, then transfer to a wire rack to cool completely.

5 To make the frosting, using an electric hand-held mixer, beat the butter, cream cheese and lemon zest and juice together. Gradually sift in the icing sugar a little at a time until a smooth frosting forms.

6 Once the cake has cooled, spread the top and sides of the cake with the frosting and decorate with walnut halves, if desired.

WHEAT, GLUTEN & DAIRY-FREE BANANA CAKE

Serves: 12

Prep: 25 mins, plus cooling

Cook: 45–50 mins

Ingredients

160 g/5¾ oz dairy-free spread, plus extra for greasing

60 g/2¼ oz brown sugar

4 tbsp maple syrup, plus extra to serve

3–4 bananas, sliced lengthways

235 g/8½ oz caster sugar

4 eggs, beaten

½ tsp vanilla extract

160 g/5¾ oz gluten-free, wheat-free self-raising flour

½ tsp xanthan gum

Method

1 Preheat the oven to 180°C/350°F/Gas Mark 4. Grease a 23-cm/9-inch round cake tin and line with baking paper. Wrap a piece of foil around the outside of the tin to prevent the syrup from leaking.

2 Heat 60 g/2¼ oz of the spread, brown sugar and maple syrup in a saucepan until the sugar melts and turns golden. Pour the mixture into the prepared tin and then arrange the sliced bananas, cut-side down, over the base.

3 Beat the remaining spread and caster sugar together in a bowl until light and creamy. Gradually add the eggs, stirring well, and the vanilla extract. Sift in the flour and xanthan gum and fold gently into the mixture. Spoon the mixture over the bananas.

4 Bake in the preheated oven for 40–45 minutes, or until risen, golden and springy to the touch. Leave to cool slightly, then invert onto a wire rack to cool completely.

FRUIT & NUT CAKES

COFFEE & WALNUT RING CAKE

Serves: 10

Prep: 20–25 mins, **Cook: 40–45 mins**
plus cooling

Ingredients

175 g/6 oz plain flour

1 tbsp baking powder

175 g/6 oz butter, softened, plus extra for greasing

175 g/6 oz light muscovado sugar

3 eggs, beaten

1 tsp coffee extract

70 g/2½ oz walnuts, chopped, plus extra walnut halves to decorate

4 tbsp maple syrup

Method

1 Preheat the oven to 160°C/325°F/Gas Mark 3. Grease a 1.5-litre/2¾-pint ring cake tin and line with baking paper.

2 Sift the flour and baking powder into a large bowl and add the butter, sugar, eggs and coffee extract. Beat well until the mixture is smooth, then stir in the chopped walnuts.

3 Spoon the mixture into the prepared tin. Bake in the preheated oven for 40–45 minutes, or until risen, golden and springy to the touch.

4 Leave to cool slightly, then transfer to a wire rack to cool completely. Whilst the cake is still warm, spoon over half the maple syrup. To serve, top with walnut halves and drizzle over the remaining maple syrup.

FRUIT & NUT CAKES

BLUEBERRY & LEMON DRIZZLE CAKE

Serves: 9

Prep: 30–35 mins, plus cooling

Cook: 1 hour

Ingredients

225 g/8 oz butter, softened, plus extra for greasing

225 g/8 oz golden caster sugar

4 eggs, beaten

250 g/9 oz self-raising flour

finely grated rind of 1 lemon

25 g/1 oz ground almonds

juice of 1 lemon

200 g/7 oz fresh blueberries

Topping

juice of 2 lemons

115 g/4 oz golden caster sugar

55 g/2 oz icing sugar

Method

1 Preheat the oven to 180°C/350°F/Gas Mark 4. Grease a 20-cm/8-inch square cake tin and line with baking paper.

2 Put the butter and caster sugar in a bowl and beat together until light and creamy. Gradually beat in the eggs, adding a little flour towards the end to prevent curdling. Beat in the lemon rind, then fold in the remaining flour and the almonds with enough lemon juice to make a dropping consistency.

3 Fold in three quarters of the blueberries and spoon into the prepared tin. Smooth the surface, then scatter the remaining blueberries on top. Bake in the preheated oven for about 1 hour, or until risen, golden and springy to the touch.

4 Meanwhile, make the topping. Put the lemon juice and caster sugar into a bowl and mix together. As soon as the cake comes out of the oven, prick it all over with a fine skewer and pour over the lemon mixture. Mix the icing sugar with a little water and drizzle over the cake. Leave in the tin until completely cool, then cut into squares.

FRUIT & NUT CAKES

FRUIT-TOPPED MADEIRA CAKE

Serves: 8-10

Prep: 25 mins, plus cooling

Cook: 1½-1¾ hours

Ingredients

25 g/8 oz butter, softened, plus extra for greasing

225 g/8 oz golden caster sugar

finely grated rind of 1 lemon

4 eggs, beaten

50 g/12 oz self-raising flour

2-3 tbsp milk

Fruit topping

2½ tbsp honey

300 g/10½ oz glacé fruit, sliced

Method

1 Preheat the oven to 160°C/325°F/Gas Mark 3. Grease a 20-cm/8-inch deep round cake tin and line with baking paper.

2 Put the butter, sugar and lemon rind in a bowl and beat together until light and creamy. Gradually beat in the eggs. Gently fold in the flour, adding enough milk to make a soft dropping consistency.

3 Spoon the mixture into the prepared tin and bake in the preheated oven for 1½-1¾ hours, or until risen, golden and springy to the touch.

4 Leave to cool slightly, then transfer to a wire rack to cool completely. To make the topping, brush the honey over the cake and arrange the fruit on top.

FRUIT & NUT CAKES

VEGAN MIXED BERRY BUNDT CAKE

Serves: 12

Prep: 25–30 mins, plus cooling

Cook: 1 hour

Ingredients

350 g/12 oz plain flour, plus extra for dusting

2 tsp baking powder

1 tsp bicarbonate of soda

400 g/14 oz caster sugar

55 g/2 oz desiccated coconut

500 ml/18 fl oz soya milk

150 ml/5 fl oz rapeseed oil, plus extra for greasing

2 tsp vanilla extract

1 tsp salt

250 g/9 oz mixed berries, such as raspberries, blueberries and blackberries, plus extra to serve

vegan icing sugar, to dust

vegan vanilla ice cream, to serve (optional)

Method

1 Preheat the oven to 180°C/350°F/Gas Mark 4. Grease and flour a 24-cm/9½-inch Bundt tin.

2 Sift together the flour, baking powder and bicarbonate of soda into a large bowl and stir in the sugar and coconut. Add the soya milk, oil and vanilla extract. Whisk together until smooth – the mixture will look like a thick batter. Stir in the salt and berries.

3 Spoon the mixture into the prepared tin. Bake in the preheated oven for 1 hour, or until risen, golden and springy to the touch. Leave to cool slightly, then transfer to a wire rack to cool completely.

4 When the cake has cooled, dust it with icing sugar and fill the centre with more fresh berries. Slice and serve with a scoop of vegan vanilla ice cream, if desired.

BLOOD ORANGE POLENTA CAKE

Serves: 8

Prep: 25 mins, plus cooling

Cook: 40–45 mins

Ingredients

butter, for greasing

250 g/9 oz cooked polenta

70 g/2½ oz soft light brown sugar

3 blood oranges or small navel oranges

Topping

4 eggs, beaten

140 g/5 oz caster sugar

150 ml/5 fl oz orange juice

1 tbsp lemon juice

125 ml/4 fl oz milk

½ tsp vanilla extract

1 tsp finely grated orange rind

Method

1 Preheat the oven to 180°C/350°F/Gas Mark 4. Grease a 23-cm/9-inch round cake tin and line with baking paper.

2 Combine the cooked polenta with 55 g/2 oz of the brown sugar in a large bowl and mix well. Spread the mixture into a thin layer in the prepared tin and bake in the preheated oven for about 20 minutes, or until it begins to colour.

3 To make the topping, whisk together the eggs, sugar, orange juice, lemon juice, milk and vanilla extract. Stir in the orange rind, then pour the mixture over the polenta base in an even layer. Bake in the preheated oven for about 15 minutes, or until the topping is starting to set. Leave the oven on.

4 Meanwhile, slice the oranges into thin rounds, using a serrated knife. Arrange the orange slices on top of the cake. Sprinkle the remaining brown sugar over the top and return the cake to the oven. Bake for a further 6–8 minutes, or until the topping is set.

5 Leave to cool slightly, then transfer to a wire rack to cool completely.

FRUIT & NUT CAKES

SUMMER FRUITS CAKE

Serves: 12

Prep: 35 mins,
plus cooling

Cook: 15 mins

Ingredients

butter, for greasing

2 firm, ripe peaches or
nectarines, or 4 apricots
or plums, stoned and sliced

55 g/2 oz soft light
brown sugar

85 g/3 oz plain flour

1 tsp baking powder

¼ tsp salt

2 eggs

1 egg white

100 g/3½ oz caster sugar

1½ tsp vanilla extract

Method

1 Preheat the oven to 190°C/375°F/Gas Mark 5. Grease a 25-cm/10-inch round cake tin and line with baking paper.

2 Put the sliced fruit into a large bowl and sprinkle the brown sugar over it. Using your hands, gently toss the fruit so that it is well coated with the sugar. Arrange the fruit in a single layer in the prepared tin.

3 Sift the flour, baking powder and salt into a small bowl. In a large bowl, whisk together the eggs, egg white and sugar with an electric hand-held mixer, until the mixture is pale and fluffy. Add the vanilla extract and whisk just to incorporate. Add the flour mixture in several additions and whisk until just combined. Spoon the mixture into the cake tin on top of the fruit, using a palette knife to spread it in an even layer. Bake for 15 minutes, or until risen, golden and springy to the touch.

4 Leave to cool slightly, then run a knife around the outside and turn it out on to a plate. Serve warm or at room temperature.

LEMON & GINGERBREAD BUNDT CAKE

Serves: 16　　**Prep: 25 mins,**　　**Cook: 30 mins**
plus cooling

Ingredients

butter, for greasing

150 g/5½ oz plain flour

150 g/5½ oz wholemeal flour

1 tbsp ground ginger

1½ tsp ground cinnamon

1 tsp salt

1 tsp baking powder

½ tsp bicarbonate of soda

125 ml/4 fl oz treacle

150 ml/5 fl oz hot water

100 g/3½ oz soft light brown sugar

100 ml/3½ fl oz rapeseed oil

85 g/3 oz unsweetened apple purée

2 eggs, beaten

Icing

100 g/3½ oz icing sugar

3 tbsp lemon juice

1 tbsp finely grated lemon rind

Method

1 Preheat the oven to 180°C/350°F/Gas Mark 4. Grease a 25-cm/10-inch Bundt tin and line with baking paper.

2 In a large bowl, sift together the flours, ginger, cinnamon, salt, baking powder and bicarbonate of soda. Put the treacle in a large heatproof bowl and pour the hot water over it, then mix until blended. Mix in the brown sugar, rapeseed oil, apple and eggs until combined. Slowly add the flour mixture, beating until combined.

3 Spoon the mixture into the prepared tin and bake in the preheated oven for about 30 minutes, or until risen and springy to the touch. Leave to cool slightly, then transfer to a wire rack to cool completely.

4 To make the icing, stir together the icing sugar, lemon juice and rind until smooth. Drizzle the icing over the cooled cake.

FRUIT & NUT CAKES

STRAWBERRIES & CREAM CAKE

Serves: 8

Prep: 50 mins, plus cooling & chilling

Cook: 40 mins

Ingredients

125 g/4½ oz butter, softened, plus extra for greasing

250 g/9 oz caster sugar

1 tsp vanilla extract

2 eggs

375 g/13 oz plain flour

2 tsp baking powder

pinch of salt

175 ml/6 fl oz milk

375 g/13 oz fresh strawberries, halved

icing sugar, for dusting

100 g/3½ oz marzipan

Buttercream filling

250 g/9 oz butter, softened

250 g/9 oz icing sugar

1 tsp vanilla extract

Method

1 Preheat the oven to 180°C/350°F/Gas Mark 4. Grease a 900 g/2 lb loaf tin and line with baking paper. Put the butter, sugar and vanilla extract into a large bowl and beat with an electric hand-held mixer until light and creamy. Add the eggs, one at a time, beating after each addition until combined.

2 Sift together the flour, baking powder and salt into a separate bowl. Gradually beat in the butter mixture, alternating with the milk.

3 Spoon the mixture into the prepared tin and bake in the preheated oven for about 40 minutes, or until risen, golden and springy to the touch.

4 Leave to cool slightly, then transfer to a wire rack to cool completely. Trim the top of the cake to make it completely flat, if necessary, then cut in half horizontally.

5 To make the buttercream, put the butter, sugar and vanilla extract into a large bowl and beat with an electric hand-held mixer until creamy. Spread half of the buttercream on top of one cake half. Place the strawberries on top of the buttercream, standing upright.

6 Cover the strawberries with the remaining buttercream, filling in any gaps in between the strawberries. Place the other cake half on top, pressing down gently but firmly.

7 Dust a work surface with icing sugar. Roll out the marzipan into a rectangle. Place on top of the cake, covering both the top and the sides.

8 Use a sharp knife to trim the edges of the marzipan. Chill the cake in the refrigerator for at least 1 hour before serving.

ALMOND CRUNCH CAKE

Serves: 8

Prep: 30 mins, plus cooling

Cook: 40–45 mins

Ingredients

150 g/5½ oz plain flour

1 tsp baking powder

½ tsp salt

125 g/4½ oz butter, melted, plus extra for greasing

1 tsp vanilla extract

5 tbsp milk

3 eggs

150 g/5½ oz caster sugar

Topping

60 g/2¼ oz butter

125 g/4½ oz caster sugar

5 tbsp whipping cream

2 tbsp plain flour

pinch of salt

85 g/3 oz flaked almonds

¼ tsp almond extract

1 tsp vanilla extract

Method

1 Preheat the oven to 180°C/350°F/Gas Mark 4. Grease a 23-cm/9-inch round cake tin and line with baking paper.

2 Sift together the flour, baking powder and salt into a large bowl. Whisk together the butter, vanilla extract and milk in a separate bowl and set aside in a warm place.

3 Put the eggs and sugar into a large bowl and beat with an electric hand-held mixer until pale and thick. Add the flour mixture and the milk mixture alternately, mixing after each addition. Spoon into the prepared tin and bake in the preheated oven for 20–25 minutes, or until risen, golden and springy to the touch. Remove the cake from the oven. Increase the oven temperature to 200°C/400°F/Gas Mark 6.

4 Meanwhile, prepare the topping. Place the butter, sugar, cream, flour and salt in a saucepan and heat over a medium–high heat, stirring, until the butter is melted. Add the almonds, bring to a simmer and cook for about 1 minute, then remove from the heat. Stir in the almond extract and vanilla extract and set aside.

5 Spread the topping on the cake. Return to the oven and bake for a further 15 minutes, until the topping is golden. Leave to cool, then serve.

FRUIT & NUT CAKES

RUM & RAISIN RING CAKE

Serves: 8

Prep: 25 mins, plus cooling

Cook: 50–60 mins, plus standing

Ingredients

150 g/5½ oz butter, softened, plus extra for greasing

150 g/5½ oz granulated sugar

4 eggs, separated

300 g/10½ oz plain flour

1 tbsp baking powder

3 tbsp rum

finely grated rind of 1 lemon

125 ml/4 fl oz milk

50 g/1¾ oz raisins

icing sugar, for dusting

Method

1 Preheat the oven to 180°C/350°F/Gas Mark 4. Grease a 24-cm/9½-inch Bundt or ring tin and line with baking paper.

2 Put the butter, sugar and egg yolks into a bowl and beat until light and creamy. Sift together the flour and baking powder into a separate bowl. Put the egg whites into a clean, grease-free bowl and whisk until they hold stiff peaks.

3 Stir the rum, lemon rind and flour mixture into the butter mixture. Add the milk and stir until bubbles form. Fold in the egg white and raisins.

4 Spoon the mixture into the prepared tin and bake in the preheated oven for 50–60 minutes. Switch off the oven, open the oven door and leave the cake in the oven for 10 minutes. Transfer to a wire rack to cool completely. Sift the icing sugar over the cake.

PECAN & COFFEE LAYER CAKE

Serves: 10–12

Prep: 30 mins, plus cooling

Cook: 20–25 mins

Ingredients

280 g/10 oz self-raising flour

1 tsp baking powder

280 g/10 oz butter, softened, plus extra for greasing

280 g/10 oz caster sugar

5 eggs

1 tbsp instant coffee granules, dissolved in 2 tbsp hot water

70 g/2½ oz pecan nuts, finely ground

chopped pecan nuts, to decorate

Frosting

450 g/1 lb cream cheese

2 tbsp maple syrup

115 g/4 oz icing sugar

Method

1 Preheat the oven to 180°C/350°F/Gas Mark 4. Grease three 23-cm/9-inch sandwich tins and line with baking paper.

2 Sift together the flour and baking powder into a large bowl. Add the butter, sugar, eggs and coffee and beat with an electric hand-held mixer until creamy. Fold in the nuts.

3 Divide the mixture evenly between the prepared tins and smooth the surfaces. Bake in the preheated oven for 20–25 minutes, or until risen, golden and springy to the touch. Leave to cool slightly, then transfer to a wire rack to cool completely.

4 To make the frosting, put the cheese and maple syrup into a bowl and beat together until well blended. Sift in the sugar and beat until the mixture is smooth.

5 Sandwich the cakes together with a third of the frosting. Spread the remainder over the top and sides of the cake and decorate with chopped pecan nuts.

FRUIT & NUT CAKES

SULTANA TEA LOAF

Serves: 10

Prep: 20 mins,
plus soaking & cooling

Cook: 40–45 mins

Ingredients

sunflower oil, for greasing

40 g/1½ oz bran flakes

115 g/4 oz sultanas

85 g/3 oz demerara sugar

300 ml/10 fl oz skimmed or
semi-skimmed milk

200 g/7 oz self-raising flour

Method

1 Grease a 450-g/1-lb loaf tin and line with baking paper.

2 Put the bran flakes, sultanas, sugar and milk into a large bowl. Cover and leave to soak for at least 1 hour in the refrigerator, or until the bran flakes have softened and the fruit has plumped up after absorbing some of the milk – the mixture can be left overnight in the refrigerator.

3 Preheat the oven to 190°C/375°F/Gas Mark 5. Stir the flour into the soaked ingredients, mix well and spoon into the prepared loaf tin. Bake in the preheated oven for 40–45 minutes, or until risen, golden and springy to the touch. Leave to cool in the tin on a wire rack.

4 When completely cool, turn the loaf out, slice and serve.

FRUIT & NUT CAKES

SPICY SQUASH KHORASAN CAKE

Serves: 8 **Prep: 30 mins,** plus soaking & cooling **Cook: 1¼ hours**

Ingredients

50 g/1¾ oz sultanas

450 g/1 lb butternut squash, peeled, deseeded and diced (prepared weight)

150 g/5½ oz butter, plus extra for greasing

150 g/5½ oz caster sugar

50 g/1¾ oz almonds, chopped

50 g/1¾ oz Italian mixed peel

finely grated rind of 1 lemon

1½ tsp ground cinnamon

1½ tsp ground ginger

85 g/3 oz khorasan flour

1 tsp baking powder

2 eggs, separated

icing sugar, for dusting

Method

1 Put the sultanas into a bowl, pour over boiling water to cover and leave to soak.

2 Preheat the oven to 180°C/350°F/Gas Mark 4. Grease a 23-cm/9-inch round cake tin and line with baking paper.

3 Put the squash and butter into a saucepan. Cover and cook over a medium heat for about 15 minutes, until soft. Tip into a bowl and beat until smooth.

4 Stir in the sugar, almonds, mixed peel, lemon rind, cinnamon, ginger and sultanas, mixing well.

5 Sift together the flour and baking powder, tipping any bran remaining in the sieve into the bowl. Gradually beat into the squash mixture.

6 Beat the egg yolks for about 3 minutes, until thick. Fold into the squash mixture.

7 Whisk the egg whites until they hold stiff peaks. Fold carefully into the mixture using a large metal spoon. Spoon the mixture into the prepared tin.

8 Bake in the preheated oven for 1 hour, or until risen and springy to the touch. Leave to cool slightly, then transfer to a wire rack to cool completely. Dust with icing sugar before serving.

GLUTEN-FREE CLEMENTINE & ALMOND CAKE

Serves: 8–10

Prep: 35 mins, plus cooling

Cook: 35–45 mins

Ingredients

125 g/4½ oz butter, softened, plus extra for greasing

125 g/4½ oz caster sugar

4 eggs, separated

150 g/5½ oz millet flour

2 tsp gluten-free baking powder

125 g/4½ oz ground almonds

juice and finely grated rind of 2 clementines

Syrup

juice of 4 clementines

100 g/3½ oz caster sugar

Topping

225 g/8 oz low-fat soft curd cheese or quark

2 tbsp sugar

2 tbsp extra-thick double cream

Method

1 Preheat the oven to 180°C/350°F/Gas Mark 4. Grease a 23-cm/9-inch round cake tin and line with baking paper.

2 Beat together the butter and sugar for 3 minutes, until light and creamy. Gradually beat in the egg yolks.

3 Sift together the flour, baking powder and ground almonds into a large bowl, then beat into the butter mixture. Mix in the clementine juice, reserving the rind.

4 Whisk the egg whites until they hold stiff peaks. Fold carefully into the mixture using a large metal spoon. Spoon the mixture into the prepared tin.

5 Bake in the preheated oven for 30–40 minutes, or until risen, golden and springy to the touch.

6 To make the syrup, put the clementine juice and sugar into a small saucepan, bring to the boil and boil for 3 minutes, until thickened.

7 Make holes all over the surface of the cake with a skewer. Pour over the hot syrup. When it has trickled into the holes, remove from the tin and transfer to a wire rack to cool completely.

8 To make the topping, beat together the curd cheese, sugar and cream. Spread over the cake and sprinkle with the reserved clementine rind.

FRUIT & NUT CAKES

COCONUT CAKE

Serves: 12

Prep: 35–40 mins, plus cooling

Cook: 25–30 mins

Ingredients

150 g/5½ oz vegetable fat

55 g/2 oz butter, plus extra for greasing

400 g/14 oz caster sugar

375 g/13 oz plain flour, plus extra for dusting

40 g/1½ oz cornflour

1 tbsp baking powder

¾ tsp salt

175 g/6 oz desiccated coconut, plus extra for decoration

225 ml/8 fl oz milk

1 tsp almond extract

½ tsp coconut extract

5 egg whites

Frosting

350 g/12 oz caster sugar

½ tsp cream of tartar

¼ tsp salt

150 ml/5 fl oz hot water

5 egg whites

½ tsp coconut extract

½ tsp vanilla extract

Method

1 Preheat the oven to 180°C/350°F/Gas Mark 4. Grease three 23-cm/9-inch round cake tins. Beat the vegetable fat with the butter using an electric hand-held mixer until fluffy. Gradually add the caster sugar, beating until light and fluffy.

2 Sift the flour, cornflour, baking powder and salt into a separate bowl and add the coconut. Add the dry ingredients to the butter mixture, alternating with the milk and 4 tablespoons of water and beating well after each addition. Stir in the almond and coconut extracts.

3 Beat the egg whites in a clean, grease-free bowl until they form stiff peaks. Fold the egg whites into the mixture until just combined. Spoon the mixture into the prepared tins and bake in the preheated oven for 20–25 minutes, or until risen, golden and springy to the touch. Leave to cool slightly, then transfer to wire racks to cool.

4 To make the frosting, heat the sugar, cream of tartar, salt and water in a saucepan, stirring constantly. In a clean grease-free bowl, beat the egg whites until they form soft peaks. Slowly add the sugar mixture, then add the coconut and vanilla extracts. Beat until stiff peaks form. Sandwich the cakes together with the frosting. Spread the remaining frosting over the cake and decorate the top with coconut.

FRUIT & NUT CAKES

BANANA CAKE WITH CARAMEL FROSTING

Serves: 12

Prep: 30 mins, plus cooling

Cook: 1 hour 5 mins

Ingredients

175 g/6 oz plain flour

1 tbsp baking powder

85 g/3 oz butter, softened

85 g/3 oz soured cream

175 g/6 oz light muscovado sugar

3 eggs, beaten

1 tsp vanilla extract

2 ripe bananas, mashed

Frosting

40 g/1½ oz butter, plus extra for greasing

40 g/1½ oz light muscovado sugar

2 tbsp soured cream

85 g/3 oz icing sugar

Method

1 Preheat the oven to 160°C/325°F/Gas Mark 3. Grease a 20-cm/8-inch square cake tin and line with baking paper.

2 Sift the flour and baking powder into a large bowl and add the butter, soured cream, sugar, eggs and vanilla extract. Beat well until the mixture is smooth. Stir in the bananas.

3 Spoon the mixture into the prepared tin. Bake in the preheated oven for about 1 hour, or until risen, golden and springy to the touch.

4 Leave to cool slightly, then transfer to a wire rack to cool completely.

5 To make the frosting, place the butter and muscovado sugar in a saucepan and simmer gently, stirring, for about 2 minutes. Remove from the heat and beat in the soured cream and icing sugar. Leave to cool for 30–40 minutes, or until thick enough to hold its shape.

6 Spread the frosting over the top of the cake, swirling with a knife.

★ **Variation**

You could also add a few drops of banana extract to the caramel frosting for a stronger banana flavour.

FRUIT & NUT CAKES

SMALL & MINI CAKES

CHOCOLATE & CHERRY CUPCAKES

Makes: 12

Prep: 25 mins, plus cooling

Cook: 25–30 mins

Ingredients

85 g/3 oz plain chocolate, broken into pieces

150 g/5½ oz self-raising flour

1 tbsp cocoa powder

2 eggs

55 g/2 oz butter, softened

3 tbsp milk

115 g/4 oz soft light brown sugar

24 fresh cherries, stoned

icing sugar, for dusting

Method

1 Preheat the oven to 180°C/350°F/Gas Mark 4. Line a muffin tin with 12 paper cases.

2 Put the chocolate in a heatproof bowl, set over a saucepan of gently simmering water and heat until melted. Leave to cool for 5 minutes.

3 Sift together the flour and cocoa powder into a bowl and add the eggs, butter, milk and brown sugar. Beat with an electric hand-held mixer for 2–3 minutes, or until smooth. Fold in the melted chocolate.

4 Spoon the mixture evenly into the paper cases. Top each cupcake with two cherries. Bake in the preheated oven for 20–25 minutes, or until risen and springy to the touch. Leave to cool slightly, then transfer to a wire rack and leave to cool completely. Dust with icing sugar just before serving.

★ Variation

To make mocha cupcakes, add 1½ tablespoons of instant coffee to the mixture at the same time as the eggs.

COFFEE FUDGE CUPCAKES

Makes: 28

Prep: 30 mins, plus cooling

Cook: 20–25 mins

Ingredients

175 g/6 oz plain flour

1 tbsp baking powder

175 g/6 oz butter, softened

175 g/6 oz caster sugar

3 eggs, beaten

1 tsp coffee extract

2 tbsp milk

chocolate-covered coffee beans, to decorate

Frosting

55 g/2 oz butter

115 g/4 oz light muscovado sugar

2 tbsp single cream or milk

½ tsp coffee extract

400 g/14 oz icing sugar

Method

1 Preheat the oven to 190°C/375°F/Gas Mark 5. Line bun tins with 28 paper cases.

2 Sift the flour and baking powder into a large bowl and add the butter, caster sugar, eggs and coffee extract. Beat well until the mixture is smooth, then beat in the milk.

3 Spoon the mixture evenly into the paper cases. Bake in the preheated oven for 15–20 minutes, or until risen, golden and springy to the touch. Leave to cool slightly, then transfer to a wire rack to cool completely.

4 To make the frosting, place the butter, muscovado sugar, cream and coffee extract in a saucepan over a medium heat and stir until melted and smooth. Bring to the boil and boil, stirring, for 2 minutes. Remove from the heat and beat in the icing sugar.

5 Stir the frosting until smooth and thick, then spoon into a piping bag fitted with a large star nozzle. Pipe a swirl of frosting on top of each cupcake and top with a coffee bean.

RASPBERRY JAM CUPCAKES

Makes: 28

Prep: 25 mins,
plus cooling

Cook: 15–20 mins

Ingredients

175 g/6 oz plain flour

1 tbsp baking powder

1 tbsp custard powder

175 g/6 oz butter, softened

175 g/6 oz golden caster sugar

3 eggs, beaten

1 tsp vanilla extract

70 g/2½ oz raspberry jam

icing sugar, for dusting

Method

1 Preheat the oven to 190°C/375°F/Gas Mark 5. Line bun tins with 28 paper cases.

2 Sift the flour, baking powder and custard powder into a large bowl and add the butter, caster sugar, eggs and vanilla extract. Beat well until the mixture is smooth.

3 Spoon the mixture evenly into the paper cases and place a half teaspoonful of jam into the centre of each, without pressing down.

4 Bake in the preheated oven for 15–20 minutes, or until risen, golden and springy to the touch. Leave to cool slightly, then transfer to a wire rack to cool completely. Dust with icing sugar before serving.

ALMOND CUPCAKES WITH POACHED PEARS

Makes: 12

Prep: 40 mins,
plus chilling

Cook: 40–45 mins

Ingredients

1.4 litres/2¼ pints water

200 g/7 oz caster sugar

6 small pears, halved, peeled and cored

1 cinnamon stick

Topping

1 egg white

2 tbsp caster sugar

¼ tsp cream of tartar

4 tbsp low-fat evaporated milk, chilled

½ tsp vanilla extract

½ tsp ground cinnamon

Almond cupcakes

85 g/3 oz ground almonds

85 g/3 oz plain flour

½ tsp baking powder

salt

25 g/1 oz butter, softened

100 g/3½ oz caster sugar

1 tsp vanilla extract or almond extract

1 egg

Method

1 To make the poached pears, put the water and sugar into a large saucepan and bring to the boil. Reduce the heat to a simmer and cook, stirring, until the sugar has dissolved. Add the pears and cinnamon stick and simmer gently for about 20 minutes until the pears are tender. Drain the pears, discarding the cooking liquor, and set aside.

2 To make the topping, put the egg white and sugar in a heatproof bowl set over a saucepan of simmering water, and whisk until the sugar has completely dissolved. Add the cream of tartar and whisk with an electric hand-held mixer for about 3 minutes or until stiff peaks form. Add the evaporated milk, vanilla extract and cinnamon and whisk until the mixture holds soft peaks. Chill until ready to serve.

3 To make the almond cupcakes, preheat the oven to 180°C/350°F/Gas Mark 4. Line a bun tin with 12 paper cases. Place the almonds, flour, baking powder and salt in a large bowl and mix to combine. In another bowl, beat together the butter and sugar with an electric hand-held mixer until light and creamy. Add the vanilla extract and the egg and beat on medium–high

speed until combined. Add half of the flour mixture and beat on medium–high speed until incorporated. Add the remaining flour and beat until incorporated.

4 Spoon the mixture evenly into the paper cases, filling each case about one third full. Bake in the preheated oven for about 15 minutes, or until the cupcakes are risen, golden and springy to the touch. Carefully take the cupcakes out of the tin, remove the paper cases and serve warm with half a poached pear and a spoonful of whipped topping.

CHERRY & ALMOND MINI LOAVES

Makes: 12

Prep: 25 mins,
plus cooling & setting

Cook: 20–25 mins

Ingredients

85 g/3 oz butter, softened,
plus extra for greasing

70 g/2½ oz caster sugar

1 egg

1 egg yolk

70 g/2½ oz self-raising flour

½ tsp almond extract

55 g/2 oz ground almonds

55 g/2 oz glacé cherries,
roughly chopped

2 tbsp flaked almonds

Icing

55 g/2 oz icing sugar

2 tsp lemon juice

Method

1 Preheat the oven to 180°C/350°F/Gas Mark 4. Place a 12-hole silicone mini loaf sheet on a baking sheet, or grease individual mini loaf tins and line with baking paper. Put the butter, caster sugar, egg, egg yolk, flour, almond extract and ground almonds into a large bowl and beat together with an electric hand-held mixer until light and creamy. Stir in the cherries.

2 Using a teaspoon, spoon the mixture into the loaf sections and smooth the surfaces. Break up the flaked almonds slightly by squeezing them in your hands and scatter them over the cake mixture. Bake in the preheated oven for 20 minutes (25 minutes if using tins), or until risen, golden and springy to the touch. Leave to cool slightly, then transfer to a wire rack to cool completely.

3 Beat the icing sugar and lemon juice together in a small bowl and drizzle over the cakes with a teaspoon. Leave to set.

BUTTERFLY CUPCAKES

Makes: 28

Prep: 35 mins, plus cooling

Cook: 15–20 mins

Ingredients

175 g/6 oz plain flour

1 tbsp baking powder

175 g/6 oz butter, softened

175 g/6 oz golden caster sugar

3 eggs, beaten

1 tsp vanilla extract

about 1 tbsp milk

coloured sprinkles, to decorate

Buttercream

100 g/3½ oz butter, softened

200 g/7 oz icing sugar

½ tsp vanilla extract

Method

1 Preheat the oven to 190°C/375°F/Gas Mark 5. Line bun tins with 28 paper cases.

2 Sift the flour and baking powder into a large bowl and add the butter, caster sugar, eggs and vanilla extract. Beat well until the mixture is smooth, then stir in enough of the milk to make a soft dropping consistency.

3 Spoon the mixture evenly into the paper cases. Bake in the preheated oven for 15–20 minutes, or until risen, golden and springy to the touch. Leave to cool slightly, then transfer to a wire rack to cool completely.

4 For the buttercream, beat together the butter, icing sugar and vanilla extract until smooth.

5 Use a serrated knife to cut a round from the top of each cupcake, then cut each round in half. Spread or pipe a little of the buttercream on top of each cake, then press the pieces of cake into it to resemble butterfly wings. Decorate with the coloured sprinkles.

SMALL & MINI CAKES

CARAMEL FUDGE WHOOPIE PIES

Makes: 10

Prep: 40 mins, plus cooling

Cook: 20–35 mins

Ingredients

250 g/9 oz plain flour

2 tsp baking powder

large pinch of salt

115 g/4 oz butter, softened

85 g/3 oz soft dark brown sugar

2 tbsp golden syrup

1 large egg

1 tsp vanilla extract

125 ml/4 fl oz milk

25 g/1 oz fudge, finely chopped

Caramel buttercream

125 g/4½ oz butter, softened

115 g/4 oz icing sugar

5 tbsp dulce de leche (caramel)

Method

1. Preheat the oven to 180°C/350°F/Gas Mark 4. Line 2–3 large baking sheets with baking paper. Sift together the plain flour, baking powder and salt in a large bowl.

2. Place the butter and sugar in a large bowl and beat with an electric hand-held mixer until light and creamy. Beat in the golden syrup, egg and vanilla extract followed by half of the flour mixture then the milk. Stir in the rest of the flour mixture and mix until thoroughly incorporated.

3. Pipe or spoon 20 mounds onto the prepared sheets, spaced well apart to allow for spreading. Bake, one sheet at a time, in the preheated oven for 10–12 minutes, or until risen and just firm to the touch. Leave to cool slightly, then, using a palette knife, transfer to a wire rack to cool completely.

4. For the buttercream, place the butter in a bowl and beat with an electric hand-held mixer for 2–3 minutes, or until light and creamy. Gradually beat in the icing sugar and continue beating for 2–3 minutes. Stir in the dulce de leche.

5. To assemble, spread or pipe two thirds of the buttercream on the flat side of half of the cakes. Thinly spread the rest of the buttercream on the tops of the remaining cakes. Sandwich the cakes together and decorate with the chopped fudge.

SMALL & MINI CAKES

RED VELVET WHOOPIE PIES

Makes: 10

Prep: 35 mins, plus cooling

Cook: 25–45 mins

Ingredients

200 g/7 oz plain flour

1½ tsp bicarbonate of soda

25 g/1 oz cocoa powder

large pinch of salt

85 g/3 oz butter, softened

85 g/3 oz white vegetable fat

150 g/5½ oz soft light brown sugar

1 large egg

1 tsp vanilla extract

1 tbsp red food colouring

150 ml/5 fl oz soured cream

Filling

250 g/9 oz cream cheese

55 g/2 oz butter, softened

few drops vanilla extract

85 g/3 oz icing sugar

Method

1 Preheat the oven to 180°C/350°F/Gas Mark 4. Line 2–3 large baking sheets with baking paper. Sift together the plain flour, bicarbonate of soda, cocoa powder and salt in a large bowl.

2 Place the butter, white vegetable fat and sugar in a large bowl and beat with an electric hand-held mixer until light and creamy. Beat in the egg, vanilla extract and food colouring followed by half of the flour mixture and then the soured cream. Stir in the rest of the flour mixture and mix until thoroughly incorporated.

3 Pipe or spoon 20 mounds onto the prepared sheets, spaced well apart to allow for spreading. Bake, one sheet at a time, in the preheated oven for 12–14 minutes, or until risen and just firm to the touch. Leave to cool slightly, then, using a palette knife, transfer to a wire rack to cool completely.

4 For the filling, place the cream cheese and butter in a bowl and beat together until well blended. Beat in the vanilla extract and icing sugar until smooth.

5 To assemble, spread or pipe the filling over the flat side of half the cakes. Top with the rest of the cakes.

GLUTEN-FREE CHOCOLATE WHOOPIE PIES

Makes: 10

Prep: 35 mins, plus cooling

Cook: 24–28 mins

Ingredients

125 g/4½ oz butter, plus extra for greasing

115 g/4 oz soft brown sugar

2 eggs, beaten

2 tsp vanilla extract

1 tsp glycerine

115 g/4 oz gluten-free, wheat-free plain flour

1 tsp gluten-free baking powder

½ tsp gluten-free bicarbonate of soda

1 tsp xanthan gum

30 g/1 oz gluten-free cocoa powder

160 ml/5½ fl oz milk

Filling

85 g/3 oz butter, softened

140 g/5 oz gluten-free icing sugar, plus extra for sprinkling

2 tbsp double cream

Method

1 Preheat the oven to 200°C/400°F/Gas Mark 6. Grease two large baking sheets and line with baking paper.

2 Beat the butter, sugar, eggs, vanilla extract and glycerine in a large bowl. Sift all the dry ingredients into the bowl and fold into the mixture. Slowly add just enough milk to make a smooth mixture.

3 Pipe or spoon 20 mounds onto the prepared sheets, spaced well apart to allow for spreading. Bake, one sheet at a time, in the preheated oven for 12–14 minutes, or until risen and just firm to the touch. Leave to cool slightly, then, using a palette knife, transfer to a wire rack to cool completely.

4 To make the filling, beat the butter, icing sugar and cream together until creamy.

5 To assemble, spread or pipe the filling on the flat side of half of the cakes. Top with the rest of the cakes. Arrange on a serving plate and sift over icing sugar.

HOME-MADE JAFFA CAKES

Makes: 12

Prep: 45 mins, plus chilling, cooling & setting

Cook: 15–17 mins

Ingredients

70 g/2½ oz orange jelly (6 cubes), finely chopped

100 ml/3½ fl oz boiling water

100 ml/3½ fl oz orange juice

2 eggs

50 g/1¾ oz caster sugar

50 g/1¾ oz plain flour

15 g/½ oz butter, melted and cooled, plus extra for greasing

150 g/5½ oz plain chocolate, broken into pieces

Method

1 Place the chopped jelly and boiling water in a heatproof bowl and stir until the jelly has dissolved. Stir in the orange juice. Line a shallow 20-cm/8-inch square cake tin with clingfilm and pour in the jelly. Chill in the refrigerator for 2 hours until set. Preheat the oven to 180°C/350°F/Gas Mark 4. Grease a 12-cup bun tin.

2 Place the eggs and sugar in a large heatproof bowl set over a saucepan of simmering water. Using an electric hand-held mixer, beat together until the mixture is thick and pale and leaves a trail on the surface when the whisk is lifted. Sift over the flour and fold in gently, then pour over the melted butter and fold in.

3 Spoon the mixture into the holes in the prepared bun tin. Bake in the preheated oven for 10–12 minutes, or until risen and golden. Leave to cool slightly, then loosen the cakes from the tin with a palette knife and transfer to a wire rack to cool.

4 Melt the chocolate in a heatproof bowl set over a pan of gently simmering water, then leave to cool slightly. Using a 4.5-cm/1¾-inch round cutter, stamp out 12 circles of jelly. Place a circle on each cake. Spoon the melted chocolate over and spread gently to cover the jelly and cake. Leave until the chocolate has set.

MINI COFFEE & MAPLE BUNDT CAKES

Makes: 4

Prep: 25 mins,
plus cooling & setting

Cook: 25–30 mins

Ingredients

115 g/4 oz butter, softened, plus extra for greasing

115 g/4 oz caster sugar

2 eggs, beaten

175 g/6 oz self-raising flour, plus extra for dusting

1 tbsp coffee and chicory essence

4 tbsp buttermilk

Icing

115 g/4 oz icing sugar

2 tbsp maple syrup

1–2 tsp water

Method

1 Preheat the oven to 180°C/350°F/Gas Mark 4. Thoroughly grease four 200-ml/7-fl oz bundt tins, then dust each with a little flour, tipping out any excess.

2 Put the butter and sugar into a large bowl and beat together until light and creamy. Gradually beat in the eggs, then fold in half of the flour. Fold in the coffee and chicory essence and buttermilk, followed by the remaining flour.

3 Spoon the mixture evenly into the prepared tins. Place on a baking sheet and bake in the preheated oven for 25–30 minutes, or until risen, golden and springy to the touch. Leave to cool slightly, then transfer to a wire rack to cool completely.

4 To make the icing, sift the sugar into a bowl and stir in the maple syrup and water, then mix until smooth. Drizzle over the cakes and leave to set.

BEETROOT BROWNIE BITES

Makes: 36

Prep: 25 mins,
plus cooling

Cook: 30–35 mins

Ingredients

150 g/5½ oz plain chocolate, broken into pieces

2 eggs

1 tsp vanilla extract

150 g/5½ oz dark muscovado sugar

85 ml/3 fl oz sunflower oil, plus extra for greasing

225 g/8 oz cooked beetroot, grated

100 g/3½ oz self-raising flour

3 tbsp cocoa powder

Method

1 Preheat the oven to 180°C/350°F/Gas Mark 4. Grease a 20-cm/8-inch square baking tin and line with baking paper.

2 Place the chocolate in a heatproof bowl, set over a pan of gently simmering water and heat until just melted. Remove from the heat.

3 Place the eggs, vanilla and sugar in a large bowl and beat with an electric hand-held mixer for 3–4 minutes, or until pale and frothy. Beat in the oil. Stir in the beetroot, then sift over the flour and cocoa and fold in. Add the melted chocolate and stir evenly.

4 Spoon the mixture into the prepared tin and bake in the preheated oven for 25–30 minutes, or until just firm to the touch. Leave to cool slightly, then transfer to a wire rack to cool completely.

5 Cut the brownie into about 36 bite-sized squares and serve.

SMALL & MINI CAKES

MINI CHOCOLATE & NUT BROWNIES

Makes: 25

Prep: 25 mins,
plus cooling

Cook: 23–25 mins

Ingredients

115 g/4 oz butter,
plus extra for greasing

100 g/3½ oz plain
chocolate, roughly
chopped

2 eggs

75 g/6 oz light muscovado
sugar

2 tsp vanilla extract

55 g/2 oz plain flour

25 g/1 oz cocoa powder

40 g/1½ oz pecan or
walnuts, roughly chopped

Method

1 Preheat the oven to 200°C/400°F/Gas Mark 6.
   Grease an 18-cm/7-inch shallow square cake tin
   and line with baking paper.

2 Put the butter and chocolate in a heatproof
   bowl, set the bowl over a saucepan of gently
   simmering water and heat until melted. Leave
   the mixture to cool slightly.

3 Put the eggs, sugar and vanilla in a large bowl
   and beat together with an electric hand-held
   mixer until the mixture begins to turn frothy.
   Stir in the chocolate mixture until combined.

4 Sift the flour and cocoa powder into the bowl
   and scatter in the nuts. Stir together gently, then
   spoon the mixture into the prepared tin.

5 Bake in the preheated oven for 18–20 minutes,
   or until the crust feels dry but gives a little when
   gently pressed. (If you're unsure, it's better to
   slightly under-cook brownies as they lose their
   gooeyness when they are over-baked.) Leave to
   cool slightly, then transfer to a wire rack to cool
   completely. Cut the brownie into 25 squares.

SMALL & MINI CAKES

APPLE & GINGERBREAD SQUARES

Makes: 24

Prep: 25 mins, plus cooling

Cook: 20 mins

Ingredients

90 g/3¼ oz butter, softened, plus extra for greasing

55 g/2 oz dark muscovado sugar

5 tbsp black treacle

1 egg white

1 tsp almond extract

175 g/6 oz plain flour, plus extra for dusting

¼ tsp bicarbonate of soda

¼ tsp baking powder

pinch of salt

½ tsp ground mixed spice

½ tsp ground ginger

125 g/4½ oz dessert apples, finely chopped

Method

1 Preheat the oven to 180°C/350°F/Gas Mark 4. Grease a small square baking tin and line with baking paper.

2 Place the butter, sugar, treacle, egg white and almond extract in a large bowl and beat with an electric hand-held mixer until smooth.

3 In a separate bowl, sift the flour, bicarbonate of soda, baking powder, salt, mixed spice and ginger together. Add to the butter mixture and beat together thoroughly. Stir in the chopped apples. Spoon the mixture into the prepared tin and smooth the surface.

4 Bake in the preheated oven for 20 minutes, or until risen and springy to the touch. Leave to cool slightly, then transfer to a wire rack to cool completely. Cut into 24 squares and serve.

SMALL & MINI CAKES

FROSTED CHOCOLATE SQUARES

Makes: 12

Prep: 20–25 mins, plus cooling

Cook: 50–55 mins

Ingredients

200 g/7 oz butter, plus extra for greasing

100 g/3½ oz plain chocolate, broken into pieces

75 ml/2½ fl oz water

350 g/12 oz plain flour

2 tsp baking powder

250 g/9 oz soft light brown sugar

75 ml/2½ fl oz soured cream

2 eggs, beaten

Frosting

200 g/7 oz plain chocolate, broken into pieces

6 tbsp water

3 tbsp single cream

15 g/½ oz butter, diced

Method

1 Preheat the oven to 190°C/375°F/Gas Mark 5. Grease a 23-cm/9-inch square cake tin and line with baking paper.

2 Melt the butter and chocolate with the water in a saucepan over a low heat, stirring frequently. Sift the flour and baking powder into a large bowl and stir in the sugar. Pour in the chocolate mixture and beat well until all of the ingredients are evenly mixed. Stir in the soured cream, followed by the eggs.

3 Spoon the mixture into the prepared tin and bake in the preheated oven for 40–45 minutes, or until risen and springy to the touch.

4 Leave to cool slightly, then transfer to a wire rack to cool completely.

5 To make the frosting, melt the chocolate with the water in a saucepan over a very low heat, stir in the cream and remove from the heat. Stir in the butter, then pour the frosting over the cooled cake, using a palette knife to spread it evenly over the top of the cake.

SMALL & MINI CAKES

MINI MANGO LOAVES

Makes: 12

Prep: 25 mins,
plus standing & cooling

Cook: 20–25 mins

Ingredients

70 g/2½ oz dried mango, finely chopped

finely grated rind of 1 orange, plus 3 tbsp juice

25 g/1 oz creamed coconut

85 g/3 oz butter, softened, plus extra for greasing

70 g/2½ oz caster sugar

1 egg

85 g/3 oz self-raising flour

icing sugar, for dusting

Method

1 Preheat the oven to 180°C/350°F/Gas Mark 4. Place a 12-hole silicone mini loaf sheet on a baking sheet, or grease individual mini loaf tins and line with baking paper.

2 Put the mango and orange juice in a small bowl and leave to stand, covered, for 2–3 hours, or until the orange juice is mostly absorbed. Finely grate the coconut (if it's very firm and difficult to grate, warm it briefly in the microwave first).

3 Put the coconut, butter, sugar, egg, flour and orange rind in a large bowl and beat together with an electric hand-held mixer until smooth and pale. Stir in the mango and any unabsorbed orange juice.

4 Using a teaspoon, spoon the mixture evenly into the loaf sections. Bake in the preheated oven for 20 minutes (25 minutes if using tins), or until risen, golden and springy to the touch. Leave to cool slightly, then transfer to a wire rack to cool completely.

5 Serve lightly dusted with icing sugar.

SMALL & MINI CAKES

ICED BABY BUNDT CAKES

Makes: 12

Prep: 35 mins, plus cooling

Cook: 15–20 mins

Ingredients

200 g/7 oz plain flour, plus extra for sprinkling

1 tsp baking powder

1 tsp ground cinnamon, plus extra for sprinkling

125 g/4½ oz caster sugar

60 g/2¼ oz walnuts, finely chopped

2 small dessert apples, peeled, cored and finely grated

6 tbsp vegetable oil, plus extra for greasing

3 eggs, beaten

150 ml/5 fl oz buttermilk

Icing

3 tbsp plain yogurt

150 g/5½ oz icing sugar

Method

1 Preheat the oven to 180°C/350°F/Gas Mark 4. Grease a 12-hole mini bundt tin and sprinkle a little flour into the holes and tilt so that both the bases and sides are coated; tap out the excess.

2 Sift the flour, baking powder and cinnamon into a large bowl. Stir in the caster sugar, walnuts and apples.

3 In a separate large bowl, beat together the oil, eggs and buttermilk. Add them to the dry ingredients and stir to form a smooth mixture.

4 Using a teaspoon, spoon the mixture evenly into the prepared tin. Bake in the preheated oven for 15–20 minutes, or until risen, golden and springy to the touch. Leave to cool slightly, then transfer to a wire rack to cool completely.

5 For the icing, put the yogurt into a bowl and add the icing sugar. Beat together well until smooth. Spoon a little of the icing onto the top of each cake, easing it slightly down the sides with the back of the spoon so the icing runs down the flutes around the sides. Lightly sprinkle the tops of the cakes with cinnamon.

CHOCOLATE & MINT CAKE POPS

Makes: 26–28

Prep: 50 mins,
plus cooling & chilling

Cook: 10 mins

Ingredients

300 g/10½ oz plain chocolate, roughly chopped

25 g/1 oz butter, softened

50 g/1¾ oz hard-boiled mint sweets

450 g/1 lb milk chocolate

50 g/1¾ oz mini marshmallows, roughly chopped

26–28 lollipop sticks

chocolate sprinkles, to decorate

Method

1 Line a baking sheet with baking paper. Put the plain chocolate in a heatproof bowl, set the bowl over a saucepan of gently simmering water and heat until melted. Stir in the butter. Leave until cool but not beginning to set.

2 Put the mint sweets in a polythene bag and tap firmly with a rolling pin until they are broken into tiny pieces. Finely chop 150 g/5½ oz of the milk chocolate, then stir it into the melted plain chocolate with the mints and marshmallows until thoroughly mixed.

3 As soon as the mixture is firm enough to hold its shape, roll 20 g/¾ oz of it into a ball. Shape the remaining cake pops in the same way. Place them on the baking sheet and chill for 30–60 minutes, or until firm but not brittle. Push a lollipop stick into each cake pop, then chill for 10 minutes.

4 Roughly chop the remaining milk chocolate and melt as above, then remove from the heat. Dip a cake pop into the chocolate, turning it until coated. Lift it from the bowl, letting the excess drip back into the bowl, and place it in a cup or tumbler. Sprinkle with chocolate sprinkles. Repeat with the remaining cake pops. Chill or leave in a cool place until the chocolate has set.

DOUBLE CHOCOLATE MINI MUFFINS

Makes: 12

Prep: 25 mins,
plus cooling

Cook: 20 mins

Ingredients

15 g/½ oz cocoa powder

70 g/2½ oz self-raising flour

¼ tsp baking powder

25 g/1 oz light muscovado sugar

85 g/3 oz milk chocolate, roughly chopped

1 egg, beaten

3 tbsp milk

40 g/1½ oz butter, melted

40 g/1½ oz plain chocolate, roughly chopped

Method

1 Preheat the oven to 190°C/375°F/Gas Mark 5. Line a mini muffin tin with 12 paper cases.

2 Sift the cocoa powder, flour and baking powder into a large bowl. Stir in the light muscovado sugar and milk chocolate. In a separate large bowl, beat together the egg, milk and butter with a fork until they are evenly combined.

3 Tip the egg mixture into the flour. Using a metal spoon, gently fold the ingredients together until only just mixed. (Don't over-mix the ingredients or the muffins won't be as light.)

4 Spoon the mixture evenly into the paper cases. Bake in the preheated oven for 15 minutes, or until risen and springy to the touch. Leave to cool slightly, then transfer to a wire rack to cool completely.

5 Put the plain chocolate in a heatproof bowl, set over a saucepan of gently simmering water and heat until melted. Using a teaspoon, drizzle the melted chocolate over the muffins.

RASPBERRY MUFFINS

Makes: 12   **Prep: 20 mins**   **Cook: 20 mins**

Ingredients

280 g/10 oz plain flour
1 tbsp baking powder
125 g/4½ oz caster sugar
2 eggs, beaten
150 ml/5 fl oz milk
100 ml/3½ fl oz sunflower oil
1 tsp vanilla extract
rind and juice of 1 small lemon
140 g/5 oz fresh raspberries
icing sugar, for sprinkling

Method

1 Preheat the oven to 200°C/400°F/Gas Mark 6. Line a muffin tin with 12 paper cases.

2 Sift the flour, baking powder and sugar into a large bowl.

3 Put the eggs, milk, oil, vanilla extract and lemon rind and juice in a separate large bowl and whisk together with a fork.

4 Stir the wet mixture into the dry ingredients and mix lightly and evenly to make a soft mixture.

5 Add the raspberries to the mixture, stirring lightly until just combined.

6 Spoon the mixture evenly into the paper cases. Bake in the preheated oven for about 20 minutes, or until risen, golden and springy to the touch. Dust with icing sugar before serving.

WARM HONEY MUFFINS

Makes: 6   **Prep: 25 mins**   **Cook: 25 mins**

Ingredients

175 g/6 oz self-raising flour

1 tsp bicarbonate of soda

55 g/2 oz clear honey

40 g/1½ oz light muscovado sugar

55 g/2 oz butter, melted, plus extra for greasing

1 egg, beaten

150 g/5½ oz Greek-style yogurt

finely grated rind of 1 small orange

warmed honey, to glaze

Strawberry salsa

2 tbsp clear honey

2 tbsp orange juice

200 g/7 oz fresh strawberries, chopped

Method

1 Preheat the oven to 200°C/400°F/Gas Mark 6. Grease six 150-ml/5-fl oz individual metal tins or six cups of a deep muffin tin.

2 Sift the flour and bicarbonate of soda into a large bowl and add the honey, sugar, butter, egg, yogurt and orange rind. Mix to combine.

3 Spoon the mixture evenly into the prepared tins. Bake in the preheated oven for 20 minutes, or until risen, golden and springy to the touch.

4 To make the strawberry salsa, warm the honey and orange juice in a small saucepan, without boiling, then pour over the chopped strawberries and stir lightly.

5 Remove the muffins from the oven, lift carefully from the tins and brush the tops with honey to glaze. Serve immediately, with the strawberry salsa on the side.

SMALL & MINI CAKES

GLUTEN-FREE BANANA MUFFINS

Makes: 12

Prep: 25–30 mins, plus cooling

Cook: 25–30 mins

Ingredients

125 g/4½ oz butter, softened

160 g/5¾ oz soft brown sugar

2 eggs, beaten

125 ml/4 fl oz single cream

2 tbsp maple syrup

1 tbsp glycerine

225 g/8 oz gluten-free, wheat-free self-raising flour

½ tsp gluten-free bicarbonate of soda

425 g/15 oz banana, mashed

Frosting

55 g/2 oz butter, softened

125 g/4½ oz gluten-free cream cheese

375 g/13 oz icing sugar

4 tbsp maple syrup, plus extra to serve (optional)

Method

1 Preheat the oven to 180°C/350°F/Gas Mark 4. Line a muffin tin with 12 paper cases.

2 Beat the butter and soft brown sugar until light and creamy. Add the eggs gradually and then slowly mix in the cream, maple syrup, glycerine, flour and bicarbonate of soda. Fold in the mashed bananas.

3 Spoon the mixture evenly into the paper cases and bake in the preheated oven for 25–30 minutes, or until risen, golden and springy to the touch. Leave to cool slightly, then transfer to a wire rack to cool completely.

4 To make the frosting, beat the butter, cream cheese, icing sugar and maple syrup using an electric hand-held mixer until smooth.

5 Place the frosting in a piping bag and pipe the frosting onto each muffin when completely cool. Serve with maple syrup if using.

MAPLE & PECAN MUFFINS

Makes: 12

Prep: 25 mins, plus standing & optional cooling

Cook: 20 mins

Ingredients

280 g / 10 oz plain flour

1 tbsp baking powder

pinch of salt

115 g / 4 oz caster sugar

100 g / 3½ oz pecan nuts, roughly chopped, plus extra pecan nut halves to decorate

2 eggs

175 ml / 6 fl oz buttermilk

125 ml / 4 fl oz maple syrup

6 tbsp sunflower oil or 85 g / 3 oz butter, melted and cooled

Method

1 Preheat the oven to 200°C/400°F/Gas Mark 6. Line a muffin tin with 12 paper cases. Sift the flour, baking powder and salt into a large bowl. Stir in the sugar and chopped pecan nuts.

2 Lightly beat the eggs in a large jug, then beat in the buttermilk, 75 ml/2½ fl oz of the maple syrup and the oil. Make a well in the centre of the dry ingredients and pour in the beaten liquid ingredients. Stir gently until just combined; do not over-mix.

3 Spoon the mixture evenly into the paper cases. Top each muffin with a pecan nut half. Bake in the preheated oven for about 20 minutes, or until risen, golden and springy to the touch.

4 Leave the muffins in the tin for 5 minutes, then brush the tops with the remaining maple syrup to glaze. Serve warm or transfer to a wire rack to cool completely.

OATY APPLE & CINNAMON MUFFINS

Makes: 12

Prep: 25 mins, plus cooling

Cook: 20–25 mins

Ingredients

200 g/7 oz wholemeal flour

75 g/2¾ oz fine oatmeal

2 tsp baking powder

1 tsp ground cinnamon

125 g/4½ oz soft light brown sugar

2 large eggs

225 ml/8 fl oz semi-skimmed milk

100 ml/3½ fl oz groundnut oil

1 tsp vanilla extract

1 large cooking apple, peeled, cored and grated

Method

1 Preheat the oven to 180°C/350°F/Gas Mark 4. Line a muffin tin with 12 paper cases.

2 Sift together the flour, oatmeal, baking powder and cinnamon into a large bowl, adding any husks that remain in the sieve. Stir in the sugar.

3 Lightly beat the eggs in a large jug, then beat in the milk, oil and vanilla extract. Make a well in the centre of the dry ingredients and pour in the beaten liquid ingredients. Stir gently until just combined; do not over-mix. Stir in the apple.

4 Spoon the mixture evenly into the paper cases. Bake in the preheated oven for 20–25 minutes, or until risen, golden and springy to the touch.

5 Leave the muffins to cool slightly, then serve warm or transfer to a wire rack to cool completely.

SMALL & MINI CAKES

VANILLA & ROSE MACAROONS

Makes: 16

Prep: 40 mins, plus standing & cooling

Cook: 10–15 mins

Ingredients

75 g/2¾ oz ground almonds

115 g/4 oz icing sugar

2 large egg whites

50 g/1¾ oz caster sugar

½ tsp vanilla extract

sugared rose petals, to decorate (optional)

Buttercream

55 g/2 oz butter, softened

¼ tsp rosewater

a few drops of pink food colouring

115 g/4 oz icing sugar

Method

1 Put the ground almonds and icing sugar into a food processor and process for 15 seconds. Sift the mixture into a bowl. Line two baking sheets with baking paper. Place the egg whites into a clean, grease-free bowl and, with an electric hand-held mixer, whisk until they hold soft peaks. Gradually whisk in the caster sugar to make a firm, glossy meringue. Whisk in the vanilla extract.

2 Using a spatula, fold the almond mixture into the meringue mixture, one third at a time, stirring to form a shiny batter with a thick ribbon-like consistency. Spoon the mixture into a piping bag fitted with a 1-cm/½-inch plain nozzle and pipe 32 small rounds onto the prepared sheets.

3 Tap the sheets firmly and let the macaroons stand for 30 minutes to let a skin form. Preheat the oven to 160°C/325°F/Gas Mark 3.

4 Bake in the preheated oven for 10–15 minutes. Leave to cool slightly, then peel the macaroons from the paper and leave to cool completely.

5 To make the buttercream, beat the butter, rosewater and pink colouring in a bowl until fluffy. Gradually beat in the icing sugar until smooth. Sandwich pairs of macaroons together with the filling and decorate with petals, if using.

MINI VICTORIA SANDWICH CAKES

Makes: 12 **Prep: 35–40 mins,** plus cooling **Cook: 15 mins**

Ingredients

70 g/2½ oz butter, softened, plus extra for greasing

70 g/2½ oz caster sugar

70 g/2½ oz self-raising flour

1 egg

1 egg yolk

1 tsp vanilla extract

To decorate

150 ml/5 fl oz double cream

6 tbsp strawberry jam

85 g/3 oz icing sugar

1 tbsp lemon juice

Method

1 Preheat the oven to 180°C/350°F/Gas Mark 4. Put a 12-hole silicone mini muffin tin on a baking sheet or grease a 12-hole mini muffin tin. Place the butter, caster sugar, flour, egg, egg yolk and vanilla in a large bowl and beat together with an electric hand-held mixer until it is smooth and creamy.

2 Using a teaspoon, spoon the mixture evenly into the prepared tin. Bake in the preheated oven for 15 minutes, or until risen, golden and springy to the touch. Leave to cool slightly, then transfer to a wire rack to cool completely.

3 To decorate, whip the cream until it just peaks. Split the cakes in half horizontally using a small serrated knife. Press 2 tablespoons of the jam through a small sieve into a bowl to extract the seeds. Put the sieved jam in a small paper piping bag and snip off the tip. Sandwich the cakes together with the remaining jam and cream.

4 Beat the icing sugar and lemon juice together in a bowl until smooth. Spoon the icing over the cakes, spreading it just to the edges. Pipe dots of jam on top of each cake and draw a wooden skewer through them.

ALMOND-TOPPED MINI SPONGES

Makes: 12

Prep: 25 mins, plus cooling

Cook: 35 mins

Ingredients

250 g/9 oz plain flour, plus extra for dusting

250 g/9 oz caster sugar

70 g/2½ oz butter, softened, plus extra for greasing

225 ml/8 fl oz single cream

1 tbsp baking powder

4 eggs

Topping

175 g/6 oz caster sugar, plus extra for sprinkling

200 g/7 oz flaked almonds

25 g/1 oz chopped almonds

1 tbsp milk

175 g/6 oz butter, melted

Method

1 Preheat the oven to 180°C/350°F/Gas Mark 4. Grease a deep 30 x 20-cm/12 x 8-inch baking tin and dust with flour, tipping out the excess. Put the flour, sugar, butter, cream, baking powder and eggs into a large bowl and beat with an electric hand-held mixer until combined. Spoon into the prepared tin and bake in the preheated oven for 15 minutes, or until risen, golden and springy to the touch. Do not switch off the oven.

2 Meanwhile, make the topping. Put the sugar, flaked almonds, chopped almonds, milk and 100 g/3½ oz of the butter into a large bowl and mix to combine. Drizzle the remaining butter evenly over the cake.

3 Use a palette knife to spread the topping evenly over the cake, then sprinkle with sugar. Return the cake to the oven and bake for a further 15 minutes. Leave to cool slightly, then transfer to a wire rack to cool completely. Cut into pieces and serve.

MINI CHOCOLATE CAKES

Makes: 9

Prep: 20 mins,
plus cooling

Cook: 20–25 mins

Ingredients

2 eggs, beaten

275 g/9¾ oz caster sugar

50 g/1¾ oz plain flour

pinch of salt

4 tbsp cocoa powder

125 g/4½ oz butter, melted,
plus extra for greasing

icing sugar, for dusting

cranberries, to decorate

whipped cream,
to serve (optional)

Method

1 Preheat the oven to 180°C/350°F/Gas Mark 4. Lightly grease 9 holes of a deep, fluted muffin tin. Beat the eggs and sugar in a large bowl, then gradually beat in the flour and salt.

2 Stir the cocoa powder into the butter and carefully stir into the mixture.

3 Spoon the mixture evenly into the prepared holes of the tin and bake in the preheated oven for 15–20 minutes, or until slightly crispy on the outside. Leave to cool slightly, then transfer to a wire rack to cool completely.

4 Dust with icing sugar, decorate with cranberries and serve with whipped cream, if using.

★ Variation

These mini chocolate cakes also taste great when served with chocolate-covered coffee beans, instead of the cranberries.

DESSERT CAKES

MOCHA CHEESECAKE

Serves: 10

Prep: 30 mins,
plus chilling & standing

Cook: 15 mins

Ingredients

85 g/3 oz butter,
plus extra for greasing

200 g/7 oz chocolate
digestive biscuits, crushed

175 g/6 oz plain chocolate,
broken into pieces

1 tbsp instant espresso
powder dissolved in
90 ml/6 tbsp boiling water

90 ml/6 tbsp cold water

6 tsp powdered gelatine

375 g/13 oz ricotta cheese

85 g/3 oz caster sugar

225 ml/8 fl oz double cream,
softly whipped

cocoa powder, to decorate

Method

1 Grease a 20-cm/8-inch round cake tin. Melt the butter in a large saucepan. Remove from the heat. Add the crushed biscuits and mix well. Spoon over the base of the prepared tin and press down evenly. Chill until firm.

2 Place the chocolate and coffee liquid in a heatproof bowl set over a pan of gently simmering water and stir until melted. Cool slightly. Pour the cold water into another heatproof bowl, sprinkle the gelatine evenly over the surface and leave for 5 minutes until spongy. Set the bowl over a pan of gently simmering water until melted. Remove from the heat.

3 Place the ricotta cheese, sugar and chocolate mixture in a large bowl, beat together with an electric hand-held mixer until smooth, then whisk in the melted gelatine. Fold in the cream then spoon over the biscuit base. Chill for at least 3 hours or until firm.

4 Dredge the top of the cheesecake with sifted cocoa powder, remove from the tin and transfer to a serving plate.

★ Variation

This cheesecake tastes great when served with coffee ice cream or mascarpone.

DESSERT CAKES

CLASSIC CHEESECAKE

Serves: 12

Prep: 35–40 mins, plus chilling & cooling

Cook: 1¼ hours

Ingredients

Base

200 g/7 oz plain flour, plus extra for dusting

4½ tbsp caster sugar

1 tsp vanilla extract

115 g/4 oz butter, softened, plus extra for greasing

1 egg

Filling

5 eggs, separated

225 g/8 oz caster sugar

800 g/1 lb 12 oz soft cheese or Quark

60 g/2¼ oz cornflour

seeds from 1 vanilla pod

300 ml/10 fl oz whipping cream

grated rind of 1 lemon

2 tbsp lemon juice

icing sugar, for dusting

Method

1 To make the base, sift the flour into a bowl and, using an electric mixer with a dough hook, beat in the sugar, vanilla extract and butter. Beat in the egg and knead to a smooth mixture. Form into a ball, wrap in clingfilm and place in the refrigerator for 1 hour.

2 Preheat the oven to 180°C/350°F/Gas Mark 4. Grease a 28-cm/11-inch round cake tin and line with baking paper.

3 Turn the dough out onto a floured surface and roll out to a thickness of about 5 mm/¼ inch. Line the base and the sides of the tin with the dough and prick the base with a fork several times. Bake in the preheated oven for about 15 minutes.

4 To make the filling, put the egg whites and sugar in a bowl and whisk until firmly peaking. In a separate bowl, beat together the cheese, cornflour, vanilla, egg yolks, cream, lemon rind and juice. Fold the whisked egg white into the cheese mixture in two stages.

5 Spread the topping onto the partially baked base and smooth flat with a spatula. Return the cheesecake to the oven for about 1 hour. Take the cheesecake out of the oven and leave to cool in the tin. Then remove from the tin and dust with icing sugar to serve.

DESSERT CAKES

CHOCOLATE CHEESECAKE

Serves: 10

Prep: 25 mins,
plus chilling

Cook: 10 mins

Ingredients

Base

115 g/4 oz digestive biscuits, crushed

2 tsp cocoa powder

55 g/2 oz butter, melted, plus extra for greasing

Filling

800 g/1 lb 12 oz mascarpone cheese

200 g/7 oz icing sugar

juice of ½ orange

finely grated rind of 1 orange

175 g/6 oz plain chocolate, melted

2 tbsp brandy

chocolate leaves, to decorate

Method

1 Grease a 20-cm/8-inch round cake tin. To make the base, put the crushed biscuits, cocoa powder and melted butter into a large bowl and mix well. Press the biscuit mixture evenly over the base of the prepared tin.

2 To make the filling, put the mascarpone cheese and icing sugar into a bowl and stir in the orange juice and rind. Add the melted chocolate and brandy and mix together until thoroughly combined. Spread the chocolate mixture evenly over the biscuit layer. Cover with clingfilm and chill for at least 4 hours.

3 Remove the cheesecake from the refrigerator, turn out onto a serving platter and decorate with chocolate leaves. Serve immediately.

BUTTERMILK CAKE WITH FUDGE ICING

Serves: 9

Prep: 30 mins,
plus cooling & setting

**Cook: 1 hour 20 mins
-1 hour 35 mins**

Ingredients

200 g/7 oz butter, softened,
plus extra for greasing

400 g/14 oz caster sugar

2 tsp finely grated
lemon rind

5 large eggs

200 ml/7 fl oz buttermilk

350 g/12 oz plain flour

½ tsp baking powder

Fudge icing

1½ tbsp golden syrup

85 g/3 oz butter

1 tbsp milk

225 g/8 oz icing sugar

1½ tbsp cocoa powder

Method

1 Preheat the oven to 180°C/350°F/Gas Mark 4. Grease a 20-cm/8-inch square cake tin and line with baking paper.

2 Place the butter, caster sugar and lemon rind in a bowl and beat with an electric hand-held mixer until light and creamy. Add the eggs, one at a time, beating well after each addition. Stir in the buttermilk. Sift over the flour and baking powder and fold in gently until thoroughly incorporated. Spoon the mixture into the prepared tin.

3 Bake in the preheated oven for 1¼–1½ hours, or until risen, golden and springy to the touch. Leave to cool slightly, then transfer to a wire rack to cool completely.

4 For the fudge icing, place the syrup, butter and milk in a large heatproof bowl set over a pan of gently simmering water. Stir until the butter has melted. Remove from the heat and sift over the icing sugar and cocoa powder. Beat until the mixture is smooth. Leave to cool for 15–20 minutes, stirring occasionally. Spread the icing over the cake and leave until set.

DESSERT CAKES

MERINGUE-TOPPED COFFEE CAKE

Serves: 6-8

Prep: 30 mins,
plus cooling & setting

Cook: 40-55 mins

Ingredients

175 g/6 oz plain flour

1 tbsp baking powder

175 g/6 oz butter, softened, plus extra for greasing

175 g/6 oz light muscovado sugar

3 eggs, beaten

1 tsp coffee extract

2 tbsp milk

3 tbsp coffee liqueur

Meringue topping

3 egg whites

150 g/5½ oz caster sugar

1½ tsp coffee extract

Method

1 Preheat the oven to 160°C/325°F/Gas Mark 3. Grease a 25-cm/10-inch round cake tin and line with baking paper.

2 Sift the flour and baking powder into a large bowl and add the butter, muscovado sugar, eggs and coffee extract. Beat well until the mixture is smooth, then stir in the milk.

3 Spoon the mixture into the prepared tin. Bake in the preheated oven for 40–50 minutes, or until risen and springy to the touch. Leave to cool in the tin for 2–3 minutes, then turn out onto a flameproof serving plate. Prick the cake all over with a skewer, then sprinkle with the liqueur.

4 To make the meringue topping, place the egg whites in a clean, grease-free bowl and whisk with an electric hand-held mixer until thick enough to hold soft peaks. Gradually add the caster sugar, whisking vigorously after each addition, then whisk in the coffee extract. Spoon the meringue on top of the cake and spread into peaks and swirls with a palette knife. Place the cake under a hot grill for 2–3 minutes, or until the meringue is just browned but still soft inside. Cut into slices and serve.

DESSERT CAKES

CHOCOLATE & CHESTNUT ROULADE

Serves: 6

Prep: 45 mins, plus cooling

Cook: 20 mins

Ingredients

6 large eggs, separated

150 g/5½ oz caster sugar

½ tsp vanilla or chocolate extract

50 g/1¾ oz cocoa powder

icing sugar, for dusting

250 ml/9 fl oz double cream

250 g/9 oz sweetened chestnut purée

2 tbsp brandy

70 g/2½ oz cooked peeled chestnuts, chopped

Method

1 Preheat the oven to 180°C/350°F/Gas Mark 4. Line a 23 x 45-cm/9 x 17¾-inch Swiss roll tin with baking paper.

2 Using an electric hand-held mixer, beat the egg yolks, caster sugar and vanilla extract together in a bowl for 10 minutes, or until doubled in volume and pale and fluffy. In a separate bowl, whisk the egg whites until they form soft peaks. Fold a tablespoonful of egg whites into the egg yolk mixture, then gently fold in the remaining egg whites and the cocoa powder.

3 Spoon the mixture into the prepared tin and smooth the surface with a palette knife. Bake in the preheated oven for 20 minutes, or until risen and springy to the touch. Leave to cool in the tin.

4 Put a large piece of baking paper over a clean tea towel and dust with icing sugar. Invert the sponge on to the baking paper and carefully peel away the lining paper. In a clean bowl, whisk the cream until stiff, then stir in the chestnut purée and the brandy. Spread over the sponge, leaving a 2.5-cm/1-inch margin around the edges, and scatter over the chestnuts. Using one end of the tea towel, carefully roll up the roulade. Dust with more icing sugar.

DESSERT CAKES

WHEAT, GLUTEN & DAIRY-FREE ROULADE

Serves: 6

Prep: 40 mins, plus cooling

Cook: 12–15 mins

Ingredients

sunflower oil, for greasing

3 large eggs

125 g/4½ oz caster sugar, plus extra to sprinkle

½ tsp almond extract

55 g/2 oz gluten-free cornflour

70 g/2½ oz ground almonds

Filling

225 g/8 oz dairy-free cream cheese

1 tbsp gluten-free icing sugar, plus extra to decorate

200 g/7 oz strawberries, hulled and sliced

Method

1 Preheat the oven to 180°C/350°F/Gas Mark 4. Grease a 20 x 30-cm/8 x 12-inch Swiss roll tin and line with baking paper.

2 Place the eggs, sugar and almond extract in a large bowl over a pan of hot, not boiling, water and whisk for about 10 minutes, until thick enough to hold a trail when the whisk is lifted. Remove from the heat and whisk in the cornflour, then fold in the ground almonds.

3 Spoon the mixture into the prepared tin and bake in the preheated oven for 12–15 minutes, or until risen, golden and springy to the touch.

4 Place a sheet of baking paper on the work surface and sprinkle with caster sugar. Invert the tin over the paper to turn out the sponge. Remove the lining paper and trim the edges from the sponge. Cover with a tea towel and leave to cool.

5 To make the filling, beat together the cream cheese and icing sugar and spread over the sponge. Top with sliced strawberries and carefully roll up from one short edge.

6 Place on a serving plate with the join underneath, and sprinkle with icing sugar to serve.

DESSERT CAKES

COFFEE & WALNUT ROULADE

Serves: 6

Prep: 40 mins, plus cooling

Cook: 12–15 mins

Ingredients

butter or oil, for greasing

3 eggs

1 egg white

115 g/4 oz golden caster sugar, plus extra for sprinkling

1 tsp coffee extract

75 g/2¾ oz plain flour, sifted

30 g/1 oz finely chopped walnuts

roughly chopped walnuts, to decorate

Filling

175 ml/6 fl oz double cream

40 g/1½ oz icing sugar, plus extra for dusting

1 tbsp coffee liqueur

Method

1 Preheat the oven to 200°C/400°F/Gas Mark 6. Grease a 33 x 22-cm/13 x 8½-inch Swiss roll tin and line with baking paper.

2 Place the eggs, egg white and sugar in a heatproof bowl set over a pan of gently simmering water. Whisk with an electric hand-held mixer until pale and it leaves a trail.

3 Whisk in the coffee extract, then fold in the flour and walnuts lightly with a metal spoon. Spoon into the prepared tin, spreading evenly. Bake in the preheated oven for 12–15 minutes, or until risen and firm to the touch.

4 Sprinkle a sheet of baking paper with caster sugar. Turn out the roulade onto the paper and peel off the lining paper. Trim the edges. Quickly roll up the sponge from one short side, with the paper inside. Leave to cool completely.

5 To make the filling, place the cream, sugar and liqueur in a bowl and whisk until the mixture begins to hold its shape. Carefully unroll the roulade, remove the paper and spread the filling over evenly. Roll up carefully.

6 Serve the roulade dusted with icing sugar, topped with roughly chopped walnuts.

DESSERT CAKES

APPLE & ALMOND ROULADE

Serves: 6

Prep: 40 mins, plus cooling

Cook: 22–27 mins

Ingredients

sunflower oil, for greasing

4 egg whites

100 g/3½ oz golden caster sugar

70 g/2½ oz ground almonds

flaked almonds, to sprinkle

ground cinnamon, to sprinkle

Filling

2 red eating apples, such as Gala, cored and chopped

1 tbsp lemon juice

140 g/5 oz fromage frais

Method

1 Preheat the oven to 200°C/400°F/Gas Mark 6. Grease a 23 x 33-cm/9 x 13-inch Swiss roll tin and line with baking paper.

2 Whisk the egg whites in a clean, grease-free bowl until stiff enough to hold soft peaks. Whisk in the sugar gradually. Fold in the ground almonds evenly with a large metal spoon.

3 Spoon the mixture into the prepared tin and bake in the preheated oven for 12–15 minutes, or until risen, golden and springy to the touch.

4 Turn the sponge out onto a sheet of baking paper on a clean tea towel and peel off the lining paper. Gently roll up the sponge from one short side, with the clean paper inside. Leave to cool completely.

5 To make the filling, place the apples in a small saucepan with the lemon juice over a high heat. Bring to the boil, cover and simmer gently, stirring occasionally, for 8–10 minutes, or until tender. Transfer to a food processor and process to a rough purée. Leave to cool.

6 Carefully unroll the roulade, remove the paper and spread evenly with the apple mixture. Top with a layer of fromage frais, then roll up loosely to enclose the filling. Sprinkle with almonds and cinnamon and serve in slices.

DESSERT CAKES

DARK CHOCOLATE ROULADE

Serves: 6–8

Prep: 45 mins, plus cooling

Cook: 20–25 mins

Ingredients

butter, for greasing

175 g/6 oz plain chocolate, broken into pieces

4 large eggs, separated

115 g/4 oz caster sugar

cocoa powder, for dusting

225 g/8 oz white chocolate, broken into pieces

225 g/8 oz mascarpone cheese or double cream

icing sugar, for sprinkling

Raspberry coulis

300 g/10½ oz raspberries

2 tbsp icing sugar

Method

1 Preheat the oven to 180°C/350°F/Gas Mark 4. Grease a 33 x 23-cm/13 x 9-inch Swiss roll tin and line with baking paper.

2 Melt the plain chocolate in a heatproof bowl set over a saucepan of gently simmering water, taking care that the bowl does not touch the water. Remove from the heat and leave to cool slightly.

3 Put the egg yolks and caster sugar into a large bowl and whisk until pale and it leaves a trail. Whisk the egg whites in a separate, clean and grease-free bowl until they hold soft peaks. Quickly stir the melted plain chocolate into the egg yolk mixture, then fold in the whisked egg whites.

4 Spoon the mixture into the prepared tin. Bake in the preheated oven for 15–20 minutes, or until risen and springy to the touch. Dust a sheet of baking paper with cocoa powder. Turn the roulade out onto the paper, cover with a clean tea towel and leave to cool completely.

5 Meanwhile, place the white chocolate in a heatproof bowl set over a saucepan of gently simmering water, taking care that the bowl does not touch the water, and stir until melted. Remove from the heat and leave to cool

DESSERT CAKES

slightly. Stir the chocolate into the mascarpone cheese, until it reaches a spreadable consistency.

6 Uncover the roulade, remove the baking paper and spread with the white chocolate cream. Use the paper to roll up the roulade to enclose the filling (do not worry if it cracks).

7 To make the raspberry coulis, put the raspberries and sugar into a food processor and process to a smooth purée. Press through a sieve to remove the pips.

8 Sprinkle the roulade with icing sugar and serve in slices with the raspberry coulis poured over the top.

FROSTED FRUITS CAKE

Serves: 16

Prep: 50–55 mins, plus cooling & chilling

Cook: 35–40 mins

Ingredients

280 g/10 oz butter, softened, plus extra for greasing

280 g/10 oz caster sugar

5 eggs, beaten

1 tbsp vanilla extract

280 g/10 oz self-raising flour

3 tbsp milk

5 tbsp raspberry or strawberry jam

150 rnl/5 fl oz double cream

350–400 g/12–14 oz summer fruits, such as strawberries, raspberries and blueberries

icing sugar, for sprinkling

Frosting

200 g/7 oz cream cheese

100 g/3½ oz butter, softened

1 tsp lemon juice

100 g/3½ oz icing sugar

pink food colouring

Method

1 Preheat the oven to 180°C/350°F/Gas Mark 4. Grease two 20-cm/8-inch sandwich tins and line with baking paper. Put the butter and caster sugar into a bowl and beat together until light and creamy. Gradually beat in the eggs, then stir in the vanilla extract. Sift in the flour and fold in gently. Stir in the milk. Divide the mixture evenly between the prepared tins and smooth the surfaces. Bake in the preheated oven for 35–40 minutes, or until risen, golden and springy to the touch. Leave to cool slightly, then transfer to a wire rack to cool completely.

2 Place one of the cakes on a flat serving plate and spread with the jam. Whip the cream until it is just holding its shape. Spread the cream over the jam, almost to the edges of the cake. Position the second cake on top and press down gently so the cream is level with the edges of the cake.

3 To make the frosting, beat together the cream cheese and butter. Add the lemon juice and icing sugar and beat until light and creamy. Beat a dash of pink food colouring into the frosting to colour it the palest shade of pink. Using a palette knife, spread a very thin layer over the top and sides of the cake to seal in the crumbs. The cake will still show through at this stage but will be

covered by the second layer of frosting. Chill in the refrigerator for
15 minutes.

4 Use the palette knife to spread a thicker layer of frosting around the sides
of the cake. Spread the remainder over the top. Once evenly covered, use
the edge of the palette knife to swirl the frosting as smoothly or as textured
as you like. Arrange the fruits on top of the cake. Put a little icing sugar in a
small, fine sieve and gently tap it over the fruits to lightly frost.

RICH CHOCOLATE TORTE

Serves: 6–8

Prep: 30–35 mins, plus cooling

Cook: 1 hour 5 mins

Ingredients

butter, for greasing

flour, for dusting

225 g/8 oz hazelnuts, skins removed

225 g/8 oz plain chocolate, 70 per cent cocoa solids

225 g/8 oz blanched almonds

5 tbsp brandy

2 tbsp strong black coffee

1 tsp ground cinnamon

2 tbsp milk

225 g/8 oz caster sugar

5 large eggs, separated

mascarpone cheese, to serve

Method

1 Preheat the oven to 180°C/350°F/Gas Mark 4. Grease a 25-cm/10-inch round cake tin and sprinkle with flour.

2 Place the hazelnuts on a baking sheet and bake in the preheated oven for 5 minutes, then leave to cool. Chop the chocolate into small pieces and place in a food processor with the almonds. Process until the mixture is like breadcrumbs.

3 Transfer the mixture to a bowl and stir in the brandy, coffee, cinnamon, milk and half of the caster sugar. Add the egg yolks, one at a time, and continue to mix.

4 Place the hazelnuts in the processor. Process until coarser than the almonds and chocolate. Add to the cake mixture and combine well. In a clean, grease-free bowl, whisk the egg whites until stiff, add the remaining caster sugar and continue to whisk. Fold the egg whites into the mixture with a large metal spoon, a few spoonfuls at a time.

5 Spoon the mixture into the prepared tin and bake in the preheated oven for 1 hour, or until risen and springy to the touch. Leave to cool slightly, then transfer to a wire rack to cool completely. Serve with mascarpone cheese.

DESSERT CAKES

RASPBERRY & CHOCOLATE TORTE

Serves: 10

Prep: 30 mins, plus cooling

Cook: 40–50 mins

Ingredients

225 g/8 oz butter, plus extra for greasing

250 g/9 oz plain chocolate, broken into pieces

1 tbsp strong black coffee

5 eggs, beaten

90 g/3¼ oz golden caster sugar

90 g/3¼ oz plain flour

1 tsp ground cinnamon

150 g/5½ oz fresh raspberries, plus extra to serve

cocoa powder, for dusting

whipped cream, to serve

Method

1 Preheat the oven to 160°C/325°F/Gas Mark 3. Grease a 23-cm/9-inch round cake tin and line with baking paper.

2 Put the butter, chocolate and coffee in a heatproof bowl set over a saucepan of gently simmering water and heat until melted. Stir and leave to cool slightly.

3 Place the eggs and sugar into a large bowl and beat until thick and pale. Gently fold in the chocolate mixture. Sift the flour and cinnamon into a bowl, then fold into the chocolate mixture. Spoon into the prepared tin and sprinkle the raspberries evenly over the top.

4 Bake in the preheated oven for 35–45 minutes, or risen and springy to the touch. Leave to cool slightly, then transfer to a large serving plate. Dust with cocoa and serve warm with raspberries and whipped cream.

DESSERT CAKES

WALNUT TORTE

Serves: 8–10

Prep: 40–45 mins, plus cooling

Cook: 25–30 mins

Ingredients

175 g/6 oz plain flour

1 tbsp baking powder

175 g/6 oz butter, softened, plus extra for greasing

175 g/6 oz golden caster sugar

3 eggs, beaten

1 tsp vanilla extract

2 tbsp milk

125 g/4½ oz walnuts, finely chopped, plus extra walnut halves to decorate

3 tbsp apricot jam, warmed

Frosting

175 g/6 oz butter

350 g/12 oz icing sugar

100 ml/3½ fl oz single cream

Method

1 Preheat the oven to 180°C/350°F/Gas Mark 4. Grease two 20-cm/8-inch sandwich tins and line with baking paper.

2 Sift the flour and baking powder into a large bowl and add the butter, caster sugar, eggs and vanilla extract. Beat until the mixture is smooth, then stir in the milk and 40 g/1½ oz of walnuts.

3 Divide the mixture evenly between the prepared tins and smooth the surfaces. Bake in the preheated oven for 25–30 minutes, or until risen, golden and springy to the touch. Leave to cool slightly, then transfer to a wire rack to cool completely. Slice each cake in half horizontally, to make four layers in total.

4 For the frosting, beat together the butter, icing sugar and cream until smooth. Spread about half of the frosting over the top of three of the cakes and sandwich them together, placing the plain one on top.

5 Spread half of the remaining frosting over the sides of the cake and press the remaining chopped walnuts over it. Brush the apricot jam over the top of the cake. Spoon the remaining frosting into a piping bag fitted with a star nozzle and pipe swirls of frosting around the top edge of the cake. Decorate with walnut halves.

DESSERT CAKES

BLACK FOREST GATEAU

Serves: 8

Prep: 40–45 mins, plus cooling

Cook: 50 mins

Ingredients

900 g/2 lb fresh cherries, stoned and halved

250 g/9 oz caster sugar

100 ml/3½ fl oz cherry brandy

100 g/3½ oz plain flour

50 g/1¾ oz cocoa powder

½ tsp baking powder

4 eggs, beaten

40 g/1½ oz butter, melted, plus extra for greasing

1 litre/1¾ pints double cream

grated plain chocolate and whole fresh cherries, to decorate

Method

1 Preheat the oven to 180°C/350°F/Gas Mark 4. Grease a 23-cm/9-inch round cake tin and line with baking paper.

2 Place the cherries in a small saucepan. Add 3 tablespoons of the sugar and the brandy and bring to a simmer. Simmer for 5 minutes. Drain, reserving the syrup.

3 In a large bowl, sift together the flour, cocoa and baking powder. Place the eggs in a heatproof bowl and beat in 160 g/5¾ oz of the remaining sugar. Place the bowl over a saucepan of gently simmering water and beat for 6 minutes, or until thickened. Remove from the heat, then gradually fold in the flour mixture and melted butter.

4 Spoon into the prepared tin and bake in the preheated oven for 40 minutes, or until risen and springy to the touch. Leave to cool in the tin.

5 Cut the cake in half horizontally. Mix together the double cream and the remaining sugar and whip lightly until soft peaks form. Spread the reserved syrup over the cut sides of the cake, then spread half of the whipped cream on the bottom half of the cake, followed by the cherries. Place the other half on top. Cover the top with the remaining cream, sprinkle over the chocolate and decorate with cherries.

DESSERT CAKES

MIXED BERRY MERINGUE CAKE

Serves: 12

Prep: 40 mins,
plus chilling & cooling

Cook: 35–40 mins

Ingredients

3 egg yolks

150 g/5½ oz caster sugar

2 tsp vanilla extract

100 ml/3½ fl oz milk

100 g/3½ oz butter,
plus extra for greasing

280 g/10 oz plain flour,
plus extra for dusting

2 tsp baking powder

Meringue topping

3 egg whites

100 g/3½ oz caster sugar

1 tsp cornflour

200 g/7 oz redcurrants,
removed from stalks

200 g/7 oz blueberries

icing sugar, for dusting

Method

1 Preheat the oven to 180°C/350°F/Gas Mark 4. Grease a 28-cm/11-inch round cake tin and lightly dust with flour. Put the egg whites in a clean, grease-free bowl and place in the refrigerator to use later in the meringue.

2 Use an electric hand-held mixer to beat the egg yolks, sugar and vanilla extract in a bowl, until fluffy.

3 Bring the milk and butter to the boil in a small saucepan over a medium heat, then pour into the egg mixture and whisk thoroughly until very thick. Sift together the flour and baking powder into the bowl and fold in gently.

4 Spoon the mixture into the prepared tin and bake in the preheated oven for 20 minutes, or until risen, golden and springy to the touch. Leave to cool slightly in the tin. Leave the oven on and turn up the temperature to 220°C/425°F/Gas Mark 7.

5 To make the topping, use an electric hand-held mixer to whisk the egg whites until they hold stiff peaks. Gradually whisk in the sugar, one tablespoon at a time, until the mixture is firm and glossy. Fold in the cornflour. Reserve 1 tablespoon

of each kind of berry and set aside. Gently fold the remaining berries into the meringue. Spread the fruity meringue mixture over the baked base.

6 Scatter the reserved berries on top of the meringue. Place the cake back in the oven and bake for a further 10–15 minutes, or until the topping is set. Dust with icing sugar when cool.

★ **Variation**

If you are having trouble finding redcurrants, you can also use gooseberries or blackcurrants.

CARAMEL PEACH GATEAU

Serves: 6–8

Prep: 35 mins, plus cooling

Cook: 25–30 mins

Ingredients

175 g/6 oz butter, softened, plus extra for greasing

175 g/6 oz light muscovado sugar

3 eggs

1 tsp vanilla extract

175 g/6 oz self-raising flour

½ tsp baking powder

2 tbsp milk

Filling

2 tbsp maple syrup

200 ml/7 fl oz crème fraîche

3 ripe peaches, thinly sliced

Method

1 Preheat the oven to 180°C/350°F/Gas Mark 4. Grease two 23-cm/9-inch sandwich tins and line with baking paper.

2 Place the butter, sugar, eggs and vanilla extract in a bowl and sift over the flour and baking powder. Beat with an electric hand-held mixer until smooth, then add the milk to make a soft consistency.

3 Divide the mixture evenly between the prepared tins and smooth the surfaces. Bake in the preheated oven for 25–30 minutes, or until risen, golden and springy to the touch. Leave to cool slightly, then transfer to a wire rack to cool completely.

4 To make the filling, swirl 1 tablespoon of maple syrup into the crème fraîche and spread half of the filling over each cooled cake.

5 Arrange half of the peach slices over one cake and sandwich with the other cake, with the filling side down. Arrange the remaining peach slices over the top of the cake.

6 Brush the top of the cake with the remaining maple syrup just before serving.

DOUBLE CHOCOLATE GATEAU

Serves: 10

Prep: 45 mins,
plus cooling & chilling

Cook: 55–60 mins

Ingredients

225 g/8 oz butter, softened,
plus extra for greasing

225 g/8 oz golden caster
sugar

4 eggs, beaten

225 g/8 oz self-raising flour

55 g/2 oz cocoa powder

a little milk (optional)

Filling

250 ml/9 fl oz whipping
cream

225 g/8 oz white chocolate,
broken into pieces

Frosting

350 g/12 oz plain
chocolate, broken into
pieces

115 g/4 oz butter

100 ml/3½ fl oz double
cream

To decorate

115 g/4 oz plain chocolate
caraque

2 tsp icing sugar and cocoa
powder, mixed

Method

1 To make the filling, put the cream in a saucepan and heat to almost boiling. Put the white chocolate in a food processor and chop. With the motor running, pour the cream through the tube and process for 10–15 seconds, until smooth. Transfer to a bowl, leave to cool, then cover and chill in the refrigerator for 2 hours, or until firm. Whisk until just starting to hold soft peaks.

2 Preheat the oven to 180°C/350°F/Gas Mark 4. Grease a 20-cm/8-inch round cake tin and line with baking paper. Put the butter and sugar in a bowl and beat until light and creamy. Gradually beat in the eggs. Sift the flour and cocoa into a bowl, then fold into the mixture, adding milk, if necessary, to make a dropping consistency.

3 Spoon into the prepared tin and bake in the preheated oven for 45–50 minutes, or until risen and springy to the touch. Leave to cool slightly, then transfer to a wire rack to cool completely.

4 To make the frosting, melt the chocolate in a heatproof bowl set over a saucepan of gently simmering water. Stir in the butter and double cream. Leave to cool. Slice the cake horizontally into 3 layers. Sandwich the layers together with the filling. Cover the top and sides of the cake with the frosting and arrange the caraque over the top. Sift the cocoa mixture over the cake.

DESSERT CAKES

GLUTEN-FREE CHOCOLATE GATEAU

Serves: 12

Prep: 35 mins,
plus cooling

Cook: 45 mins

Ingredients

90 g/3¼ oz gluten-free cocoa powder, plus extra for dusting

175 g/6 oz butter, plus extra for greasing

240 ml/8½ fl oz strong black coffee

200 g/7 oz caster sugar

120 g/4¼ oz gluten-free, wheat-free plain flour

1 tsp gluten-free baking powder

1 tsp gluten-free bicarbonate of soda

¼ tsp xanthan gum

pinch of salt

2 eggs, beaten

125 g/4½ oz plain yogurt

1 tbsp raspberry liqueur

1 tsp vanilla extract

Frosting

175 g/6 oz caster sugar

600 ml/1 pint double cream

2 punnets raspberries, washed, to decorate

Method

1 Preheat the oven to 180°C/350°F/Gas Mark 4. Grease two 23-cm/9-inch round cake tins and line with baking paper.

2 Put the cocoa powder, butter and the coffee into a saucepan and simmer until the butter has melted. Remove from the heat, mix in the sugar and leave to one side to cool slightly.

3 In a large bowl, mix the flour, baking powder, bicarbonate of soda, xanthan gum and salt together. Add the flour mixture to the cocoa mixture in the pan and stir in until combined. Gradually add the eggs and mix well. Add the yogurt, raspberry liqueur and vanilla extract and stir well.

4 Divide the mixture evenly between the prepared tins and smooth the surfaces. Bake for 40 minutes, or until risen and springy to the touch. Leave to cool slightly, then transfer to a wire rack to cool completely.

5 To make the frosting, whip together the sugar and cream in a large bowl. Use half of the cream mixture and half of the raspberries to sandwich the cakes together and then spread the remaining half of the cream on top of the cake, and decorate with the remaining raspberries.

RICH WALNUT CAKE WITH MAPLE SAUCE

Serves: 9 **Prep: 25 mins,** plus cooling **Cook: 45–55 mins**

Ingredients

175 g/6 oz plain flour

1 tbsp baking powder

175 g/6 oz butter, softened, plus extra for greasing

175 g/6 oz light muscovado sugar

3 eggs, beaten

1 tsp coffee extract

2 tbsp crème fraîche

55 g/2 oz walnuts, finely chopped, plus extra walnut halves to decorate

Sauce

4 tbsp crème fraîche

3 tbsp maple syrup

Method

1 Preheat the oven to 160°C/325°F/Gas Mark 3. Grease a 23-cm/9-inch square cake tin and line with baking paper.

2 Sift the flour and baking powder into a large bowl and add the butter, sugar, eggs and coffee extract. Beat well until the mixture is smooth, then stir in the crème fraîche and chopped walnuts.

3 Spoon the mixture into the prepared tin. Bake in the preheated oven for 40–50 minutes, or until risen, golden and springy to the touch.

4 Leave to cool slightly, then transfer to a serving plate. Cut into nine squares. Place the crème fraîche and maple syrup in a small saucepan and heat gently, stirring until melted and smooth.

5 Top each square of cake with a walnut half, spoon over the warm sauce and serve immediately.

BLUEBERRY SWIRL GATEAU

Serves: 8–10

Prep: 35 mins,
plus cooling

Cook: 20–25 mins

Ingredients

175 g/6 oz plain flour

1 tbsp baking powder

175 g/6 oz butter, softened,
plus extra for greasing

175 g/6 oz caster sugar

3 eggs, beaten

1 tsp orange flower water

2 tbsp orange juice

Frosting

200 g/7 oz cream cheese

100 g/3½ oz icing sugar

225 g/8 oz fresh blueberries

Method

1 Preheat the oven to 160°C/325°F/Gas Mark 3. Grease three 20-cm/8-inch sandwich tins and line with baking paper.

2 Sift the flour and baking powder into a large bowl and add the butter, caster sugar, eggs and orange flower water. Beat well until the mixture is smooth, then stir in the orange juice.

3 Divide the mixture evenly between the prepared tins and smooth the surfaces. Bake in the preheated oven for 20–25 minutes, or until risen, golden and springy to the touch. Leave to cool slightly, then transfer to a wire rack to cool completely.

4 To make the frosting, beat together the cream cheese and icing sugar until smooth. Transfer about two thirds of the mixture to a separate bowl and stir in 140 g/5 oz of the blueberries, then use this to sandwich the three cakes together.

5 Rub the remaining blueberries through a fine sieve to make a smooth purée. Spread the remaining frosting on top of the cake and swirl the blueberry purée through it.

DESSERT CAKES

MOCHA SPONGE PUDDINGS

Makes: 6　　　　　**Prep: 25 mins**　　　　　**Cook: 25–30 mins**

Ingredients

175 g/6 oz plain flour

2 tbsp cocoa powder

2 tsp baking powder

175 g/6 oz butter, softened, plus extra for greasing

175 g/6 oz light muscovado sugar

3 eggs, beaten

1 tsp coffee extract

6 small squares of plain chocolate

Sauce

250 ml/9 fl oz single cream

100 g/3½ oz plain chocolate, broken into pieces

1 tsp coffee extract

Method

1 Preheat the oven to 200°C/400°F/Gas Mark 6. Grease six 200-ml/7-fl oz metal pudding basins.

2 Sift the flour, cocoa and baking powder into a large bowl and add the butter, sugar, eggs and coffee extract. Beat well until the mixture is smooth.

3 Spoon the mixture into the prepared pudding basins. Place a square of chocolate on top of each. Bake in the preheated oven for 20–25 minutes, or until risen and springy to the touch.

4 To make the sauce, place the cream, chocolate and coffee extract in a small saucepan and heat gently without boiling, stirring, until melted and smooth. Turn out the puddings and serve with the sauce poured over them.

LEMON DESSERT CAKES

Makes: 6

Prep: 20 mins,
plus cooling

Cook: 30–35 mins

Ingredients

175 g/6 oz plain flour

1 tbsp baking powder

175 g/6 oz butter, softened,
plus extra for greasing

175 g/6 oz caster sugar

3 eggs, separated

finely grated rind and
juice of 2 lemons

150 ml/5 fl oz milk

Method

1 Preheat the oven to 180°C/350°F/Gas Mark 4.
Grease six 200-ml/7-fl oz ovenproof teacups or
ramekins and place in a roasting tin.

2 Sift the flour and baking powder into a large
bowl and add the butter, sugar and egg yolks.
Beat well until the mixture is smooth, then stir in
the lemon rind, lemon juice and milk. In a clean,
grease-free bowl, whisk the egg whites until they
hold stiff peaks. Fold into the butter mixture.

3 Divide the mixture evenly between the prepared
teacups. Pour enough hot water into the tin to
come halfway up the sides of the teacups. Bake
in the preheated oven for 30–35 minutes, or until
risen, golden and springy to the touch.

4 Leave to cool slightly, then transfer the teacups
to warmed serving plates.

DESSERT CAKES

ALMOND & HAZELNUT GATEAU

Serves: 8

Prep: 30 mins,
plus cooling, setting
& chilling

Cook: 15–20 mins

Ingredients

4 eggs

115 g/4 oz caster sugar

50 g/1¾ oz ground almonds

50 g/1¾ oz ground hazelnuts

50 g/1¾ oz plain flour

70 g/2½ oz flaked almonds

icing sugar, for dusting

Filling

100 g/3½ oz plain chocolate, broken into pieces

1 tbsp butter, plus extra for greasing

300 ml/10 fl oz double cream

Method

1 Preheat the oven to 190°C/375°F/Gas Mark 5. Grease two 18-cm/7-inch sandwich tins and line with baking paper.

2 Whisk the eggs and caster sugar in a large bowl with an electric hand-held mixer for about 10 minutes, or until the mixture is very light and a trail is left when the whisk is dragged across the surface. Fold in the ground nuts. Sift the flour and fold in with a metal spoon or palette knife. Divide the mixture evenly between the prepared tins.

3 Scatter the flaked almonds over one of the cakes. Bake both of the cakes in the preheated oven for 15–20 minutes, or until risen and springy to the touch. Leave to cool slightly, then transfer to a wire rack to cool completely. Meanwhile, make the filling. Melt the chocolate in a heatproof bowl set over a saucepan of gently simmering water. Remove from the heat and stir in the butter. Leave the mixture to cool slightly. Whip the cream until just holding its shape, then fold in the melted chocolate mixture.

4 Place the cake without the extra almonds on a serving plate and spread the filling over it. Leave the filling to set slightly, then place the almond-topped cake on top and chill for about 1 hour. Dust with icing sugar.

DESSERT CAKES

CHOCOLATE TRUFFLE TORTE

Serves: 10

Prep: 40 mins,
plus cooling & chilling

Cook: 12–15 mins

Ingredients

butter, for greasing

50 g/1¾ oz caster sugar

2 eggs, beaten

40 g/1½ oz plain flour

25 g/1 oz cocoa powder

4 tbsp strong coffee

2 tbsp brandy

cocoa powder and icing sugar, for dusting

Truffle topping

600 ml/1 pint whipping cream

425 g/15 oz plain chocolate, broken into pieces

Method

1 Preheat the oven to 220°C/425°F/Gas Mark 7. Grease a 23-cm/9-inch round cake tin and line with baking paper.

2 Put the caster sugar and eggs in a heatproof bowl set over a saucepan of gently simmering water. Whisk together until pale and resembling the texture of mousse. Sift in the flour and cocoa and fold gently into the mixture. Spoon into the prepared tin and bake in the preheated oven for 7–10 minutes, or until risen and springy to the touch.

3 Leave to cool slightly, then transfer to a wire rack to cool completely. Wash and dry the tin and replace the cooled cake in the tin. Mix together the coffee and brandy and brush over the cake.

4 To make the truffle topping, put the cream in a bowl and whisk until just holding very soft peaks. Put the chocolate in a heatproof bowl set over a saucepan of gently simmering water until melted. Carefully fold the cooled melted chocolate into the cream. Pour the chocolate mixture over the sponge. Chill until set.

5 To decorate, sift cocoa over the top and remove carefully from the tin. Using strips of baking paper, sift bands of icing sugar over the torte to create a striped pattern.

DESSERT CAKES

WARM WHITE CHOCOLATE & MACADAMIA RING

Serves: 8

Prep: 25 mins, plus cooling

Cook: 45–50 mins

Ingredients

70 g/2½ oz white chocolate, broken into pieces

2 tbsp milk

1 tsp vanilla extract

175 g/6 oz plain flour

1 tbsp baking powder

175 g/6 oz butter, softened, plus extra for greasing

175 g/6 oz caster sugar

3 eggs, beaten

55 g/2 oz macadamia nuts, finely chopped, plus extra to decorate

Sauce

100 g/3½ oz white chocolate, broken into pieces

125 ml/4 fl oz single cream

½ tsp vanilla extract

Method

1 Preheat the oven to 180°C/350°F/Gas Mark 4. Grease a 1.5-litre/2¾-pint ring tin and line with baking paper.

2 Place the chocolate, milk and vanilla extract in a small saucepan and heat gently, stirring occasionally, until just melted and smooth. Remove from the heat.

3 Sift the flour and baking powder into a large bowl and add the butter, sugar and eggs. Beat well until the mixture is smooth, then beat in the melted chocolate mixture. Stir in the macadamia nuts, mixing evenly.

4 Spoon the mixture into the prepared tin. Bake in the preheated oven for 35–40 minutes, or until risen, golden and springy to the touch. Leave to cool slightly, then transfer to a warmed serving plate.

5 For the sauce, place the chocolate, cream and vanilla extract in a saucepan and heat gently until melted and smooth.

6 Drizzle the sauce over the cake and sprinkle with the macadamia nuts, then serve warm.

COCONUT MERINGUE CAKE

Serves: 6–8

Prep: 30 mins,
plus cooling

Cook: 20–30 mins

Ingredients

140 g/5 oz butter, softened, plus extra for greasing

175 g/6 oz caster sugar

3 egg yolks

2 tsp vanilla extract

250 g/9 oz plain flour

2 tsp baking powder

225 g/8 oz raspberry jam

Meringue topping

3 egg whites

pinch of salt

60 g/2¼ oz caster sugar

85 g/3 oz desiccated coconut

1 tsp vanilla extract

Method

1 Preheat the oven to 180°C/350°F/Gas Mark 4. Grease a 20-cm/8-inch round cake tin and line with baking paper.

2 Put the butter and sugar into a large bowl and beat until light and creamy. Add the egg yolks and beat until incorporated. Add the vanilla extract, then fold in the flour and baking powder. The mixture should be quite crumbly in texture.

3 Spoon the mixture into the prepared tin and bake in the preheated oven for 10–15 minutes, or until risen, golden and springy to the touch. Leave the oven on as you will need it to cook the meringue topping.

4 Remove the cake from the oven and use a palette knife to spread the jam over the entire surface of the cake.

5 To make the topping, put the egg whites into a clean, grease-free bowl with the salt and whisk until they hold soft peaks. Using a wooden spoon, carefully fold in the sugar and coconut. Add the vanilla extract and lightly stir to incorporate. Use a palette knife to spread the meringue over the top of the jam-covered cake.

6 Bake in the preheated oven again for a further 10–15 minutes, or until the meringue is a light

golden brown. Make sure that the meringue doesn't burn. Leave to cool slightly, then transfer to a wire rack to cool completely.

★ Variation

You can try making this cake with a variety of different jams; both strawberry or blackberry jam would work well with the flavours in this cake.

INDEX

INDEX

This edition published by Parragon Books Ltd in 2014
LOVE FOOD is an imprint of Parragon Books Ltd

Parragon Books Ltd
Chartist House
15–17 Trim Street
Bath BA1 1HA, UK
www.parragon.com/lovefood

ISBN 978-1-4723-6347-3
Printed in China

Introduction by Anne Sheasby

Bundt ® is a registered trade mark of Northland Aluminium Products, Inc.

Notes for the Reader
This book uses both metric and imperial measurements. Follow the
same units of measurement throughout; do not mix metric and imperial.
All spoon measurements are level: teaspoons are assumed to be 5 ml,
and tablespoons are assumed to be 15 ml. Unless otherwise stated, milk
is assumed to be full fat, eggs and individual vegetables are medium,
and pepper is freshly ground black pepper. Unless otherwise stated, all
root vegetables should be peeled prior to using.

Garnishes, decorations and serving suggestions are all optional and
not necessarily included in the recipe ingredients or method. The
times given are an approximate guide only. Preparation times differ
according to the techniques used by different people and the cooking
times may also vary from those given. Optional ingredients, variations or
serving suggestions have not been included in the time calculations.

150 Recipes series

150
BAKING
recipes
INSPIRED IDEAS FOR
EVERYDAY COOKING

150
CAKE
recipes
INSPIRED IDEAS FOR
EVERYDAY COOKING

150
CHICKEN
recipes
INSPIRED IDEAS FOR
EVERYDAY COOKING

150
CUPCAKE
& MUFFIN
recipes
INSPIRED IDEAS FOR
EVERYDAY COOKING

150
FAST
& SIMPLE
recipes
INSPIRED IDEAS FOR
EVERYDAY COOKING

150
INDIAN
recipes
INSPIRED IDEAS FOR
EVERYDAY COOKING

150
PASTA
recipes
INSPIRED IDEAS FOR
EVERYDAY COOKING

150
SLOW
COOKER
recipes
INSPIRED IDEAS FOR
EVERYDAY COOKING

150
STIR-FRY
recipes
INSPIRED IDEAS FOR
EVERYDAY COOKING

150
STUDENT
recipes
INSPIRED IDEAS FOR
EVERYDAY COOKING

150
TAPAS
recipes
INSPIRED IDEAS FOR
EVERYDAY COOKING

150
VEGETARIAN
recipes
INSPIRED IDEAS FOR
EVERYDAY COOKING